Stopping Oil

'*Stopping Oil* follows the entanglement of racial capitalism, colonialism and Western modernity that situates resource extraction in Aotearoa New Zealand. And, crucially, drawing on the authors' own experiences of direct action and resistance, it also outlines a hopeful ethics of care through which meaningful changes can be achieved.'

—Jo Sharp, Professor of Geography, University of St Andrews

'Documents an important period of climate activism in Aotearoa New Zealand, with wider relevance for democratic activism. It connects direct action with a feminist ethics and politics of care, with theoretical relevance for students and activists far beyond these shores.'

—Kelly Dombroski, an editor of *New Zealand Geographer*

Radical Geography

Series Editors:
Danny Dorling, Matthew T. Huber and Jenny Pickerill
Former editor: Kate Derickson

Also available:

Disarming Doomsday:
The Human Impact of Nuclear Weapons since Hiroshima
Becky Alexis-Martin

Unlocking Sustainable Cities:
A Manifesto for Real Change
Paul Chatterton

In Their Place:
The Imagined Geographies of Poverty
Stephen Crossley

Geographies of Digital Exclusion:
Data and Inequality
Mark Graham and Martin Dittus

Making Workers:
Radical Geographies of Education
Katharyne Mitchell

Space Invaders:
Radical Geographies of Protest
Paul Routledge

Data Power:
Radical Geographies of Control and Resistance
Jim E. Thatcher and Craig M. Dalton

New Borders:
Hotspots and the European Migration Regime
Antonis Vradis, Evie Papada, Joe Painter and Anna Papouts

Stopping Oil

Climate Justice and Hope

Sophie Bond, Amanda Thomas
and Gradon Diprose

PLUTO PRESS

First published 2023 by Pluto Press
New Wing, Somerset House, Strand, London WC2R 1LA
and Pluto Press Inc.
1930 Village Center Circle, 3-834, Las Vegas, NV 89134

www.plutobooks.com

British Library Cataloguing in Publication Data
A catalogue record for this book is available from the British Library

ISBN   978 0 7453 4131 6   Paperback
ISBN   978 1 786808 22 6   PDF
ISBN   978 1 786808 23 3   EPUB

This book is printed on paper suitable for recycling and made from fully
managed and sustained forest sources. Logging, pulping and manufacturing
processes are expected to conform to the environmental standards of the
country of origin.

Typeset by Stanford DTP Services, Northampton, England

Simultaneously printed in the United Kingdom and United States of America

Contents

Series Preface

The Radical Geography series consists of accessible books which use geographical perspectives to understand issues of social and political concern. These short books include critiques of existing government policies and alternatives to staid ways of thinking about our societies. They feature stories of radical social and political activism, guides to achieving change, and arguments about why we need to think differently on many contemporary issues if we are to live better together on this planet.

A geographical perspective involves seeing the connections within and between places, as well as considering the role of space and scale to develop a new and better understanding of current problems. Written largely by academic geographers, books in the series deliberately target issues of political, environmental and social concern. The series showcases clear explications of geographical approaches to social problems, and it has a particular interest in action currently being undertaken to achieve positive change that is radical, achievable, real and relevant.

The target audience ranges from undergraduates to experienced scholars, as well as from activists to conventional policy-makers, but these books are also for people interested in the world who do not already have a radical outlook and who want to be engaged and informed by a short, well written and thought-provoking book.

Danny Dorling, Matthew T. Huber and Jenny Pickerill
Series Editors

Acknowledgements

We're grateful to our research participants and communities across Aotearoa New Zealand and elsewhere who continue to work towards climate justice. He mihi maioha, warm thanks to Terence Hikawai for helping us with the glossary of Māori terms. We've worked with some brilliant postgraduate students and research assistants along the way – there were many, but specifically Sonja Bohn, Jule Barth and Heather Urquhart have made significant contributions across data collection, analysis and editing. Thank you all for your care and energy in this project. Thank you to Jenny Pickerill for encouraging us to write this book and for her generous feedback and suggestions on earlier drafts. And thank you to our families for their constant support.

Glossary of Te Reo Māori Terms

These translations are derived from Fitzmaurice and Bargh (2022), the Waitangi Tribunal (e.g. 1996, 2003, 2011, 2015), Te Aka – https://maoridictionary.co.nz/, and other sources, with input from Terence Hikawai. The definitions are not exhaustive, but are related to the context the terms are used in this book.

Aotearoa – Māori name originally for the North Island, now used to refer to the whole country that is also known as New Zealand. In this text, we typically write Aotearoa New Zealand to reflect the (post)colonial status

atua – gods, ancestor, deity

hapū – kinship group, clan, subtribe

iwi – tribe, kinship group

kaitiakitanga – guardianship and care that Māori have toward the environment within their territory, territory that they are genealogically connected to

kāwanatanga – government, often more specifically government by the Crown, governorship

mana – authority, power, influence, jurisdiction

mātauranga – wisdom, knowledge rooted in te ao Māori

Pākehā – white New Zealanders of European descent

rangatiratanga – authority that comes from people, land, ancestors and the spiritual realm, often equated with sovereignty or self-determination but goes beyond these concepts and is specific to Māoridom

rohe moana – territories at sea and lakes, areas that an iwi or hapū have authority to

tangata whenua – Indigenous people, local peoples, tied to a place

taonga – resources or possessions, anything prized

tapu – sacred, a supernatural state, restrictions

te ao Māori – the Māori world and ways of doing things

te reo Māori – the Māori language

tika – to be right, just, fair, correct

tikanga – lore, custom, correct conduct, values, practices

tino rangatiratanga – absolute authority, autonomy
tipua – uncanny spiritual things
wairua – spirit, soul
whakapapa – genealogy, lineage, ancestry

1

Security for Whom?

Between 2008 and 2017 Aotearoa New Zealand's offshore environment was opened up for further oil and gas exploration on the promise of economic growth and energy independence. The dominant narrative from the government and from industry was, at its core, that economic growth is essential, that oil was an untapped resource, and it would be irresponsible not to make use of it to generate capital and contribute to Aotearoa New Zealand's economic development. During these nine years, the government sought to 'secure' this resource. It embarked on actions to provide certainty and therefore security for overseas investors by cultivating ties with the fossil fuel industry. When protest sought to disrupt oil and gas exploration activities that had been secured, the government introduced legislation to curtail at-sea protest and offered only limited Māori and community engagement about commercial extraction activities in ocean spaces. The so-called Anadarko Amendment (discussed in Chapter 3) is perhaps most symbolic of this approach. The Amendment contravened international human rights law, and went against a long tradition of protest at sea in Aotearoa New Zealand, by banning activists from coming within 500 m of an oil and gas vessel (Pender and MacMillan 2013). The Minister for Energy and Resources at the time said the protesters shouldn't be trying to 'stop other people going about their lawful business' (TVNZ 2013).

But this period also saw a rise of Māori- and community-led activism against the extractive economy, and the formation and deepening of connections between people and groups seeking to protect communities and environments. While the Anadarko Amendment sought to provide assurances and security to fossil fuel companies, activists changed the financial equation by disrupting exploration, blockading banks who refused to divest from oil and gas, and protesting annual fossil fuel conferences. Activists sought to secure a future that was not dependent on fossil fuels, and that both demanded and demonstrated a sense of responsibility and care for the impacts of continuing business-as-usual.

This book is the story of a climate justice campaign to stop deep sea oil exploration and drilling in Aotearoa New Zealand. It documents the push-pull of the Oil Free campaign and various tactics by the media, the government and the petroleum industry. It documents the ways in which the government and industry engaged in tactics to narrow down or close off the spaces of dissent and protest, as they tried to secure and develop the petroleum economy in the Exclusive Economic Zone (EEZ) of Aotearoa New Zealand. The book also highlights how climate activists navigated this closure to secure a different, more climate-just, vision of the future. We situate this story within ideas of environmental democracy, where democracy is understood as the ability to engage in active and robust debate about issues and the ability to meaningfully dissent, be heard, and propose ideas for alternative futures that are more fair, just and sustainable. Therefore, the story we tell is not unique even though it is situated in the specific context of a small OECD country in the South Pacific. It speaks to patterns of environmental politics that are refracted elsewhere, at a moment in which it is hard to understand just why change is so difficult when the science is so clear. The purpose of this book is to highlight some of the practices, labour and tactics involved in maintaining business-as-usual, and the work involved in shifting trajectories.

In early 2018, a newly elected government enacted legislation that banned all new oil and gas exploration permits in Aotearoa's EEZ with the exception of an area of active production off the west coast of the North Island in Taranaki. At the time, media debate was polemic, either decrying the lost revenue and the impact it would have on the economy, or arguing it didn't go far enough because it did not apply to existing permits. At the beginning of 2021, the last existing exploration permit was surrendered. While we don't suggest that these actions, or those of the current government in relation to climate change are anywhere near enough, we argue that the Oil Free campaign disrupted efforts made to secure the resource for investors in the 'blue frontier' of Aotearoa New Zealand's EEZ.

THE VALUE OF A STORY IN AOTEAROA NEW ZEALAND

In feedback on our research, we're often asked to justify why international readers 'should care' about the specific case study of Aotearoa New

Zealand. This sort of feedback goes to the heart of the colonial logics that continue to pervade academia. Case studies that are distant (spatially, perhaps culturally) from the supposed heartlands of geography and theory are either just that – case studies rather than locations of theory production – or need to be justified in their otherness. We're reluctant to engage in such justifications again in this space; theory comes from here and this is a dynamic, useful case study for climate justice in a multitude of ways. Aotearoa New Zealand melds together ongoing colonialism, rapid and deep neoliberal reform and experimentation, and a history of activism for Māori land rights, the anti-nuclear movement in Oceania, through to enormous turnouts for recent student climate strikes (for instance, 3.4 per cent of the whole population in March 2019). Like all case studies, this one is riven with contradictions, mundane bureaucratic moves with outsized impacts, and fascinating communities and people. In carrying out fieldwork over four years, we were able to talk to over 50 people engaged in climate justice or Oil Free activism, engage in some ourselves, and speak with a few people who worked in the oil and gas industry. We also carried out an analysis of media reporting. Much of this research has been published elsewhere in academic journals, as well as a findings report. We have also drawn on this work in submissions in government processes, and in media articles. This book takes a different approach with the purpose of sharing the story as a whole, linking key ideas, and more explicitly situating the story of this campaign within a broader trajectory of climate justice.

In thinking and writing about climate justice in Aotearoa New Zealand, it's also necessary to more specifically locate ourselves. All three of us are Pākehā, white New Zealanders of European descent. Colonialism is a dogged structure blocking the way to climate justice, and shaping knowledge production. It is a structure that we three benefit from, particularly working in research and tertiary institutions, and a structure that we try to challenge. This book draws together our research experience, and hopefully builds on the work of Māori communities and scholars who have forged the way in defining a decolonised climate justice for this place (Bargh 2019; Bargh and Tapsell 2021; Ruckstuhl et al. 2013; see also the work of Shaun Awatere, Emily Tuhi-Ao Bailey, Lyn Carter, Nadine Anne Hura, Merata Kawharu, Sandy Morrison, Naomi Simmonds, Huhana Smith, and Dayle Takitimu. This is not by any means an exhaustive list).

FEMINIST GEOGRAPHIES AND CLIMATE JUSTICE

There is a huge range of ways to approach climate activism and its different components. Others have written about communication, different tactics and strategies in activism, the origins of climate justice language, Indigenous communities' leadership, how it's shaped policy, and the messiness of organising (Whyte 2017a; Matthews 2020; Oosterman 2018). In this book, we take a feminist political geography perspective. This means that we understand politics and activism to be happening at every scale, and that one isn't more important than another. So, for example, in Chapter 3, we discuss some of the things happening in an international context that spurred on activism here, while also later discussing the way individuals feel anxieties about climate change, or build friendships with each other to enable them to sustain their activism (see Chapter 7). Feminist political geographies also question how issues are experienced by different people. For instance, in Chapter 5, we write about ideas of security. Feminist geopolitics have pointed out that we need to ask *who* is being made secure. When it comes to climate change, this goes to the heart of demands for climate justice; carbon emissions and climate change impacts are very uneven. A recent report pointed out that the richest 10 per cent of people were responsible for 52 per cent of carbon emissions between 1990 and 2015 (Oxfam 2020). But it is working-class people, those with insecure housing, those who can't afford heating and cooling systems, or who live on marginal land exposed to hurricanes, for example, who will suffer the worst impacts of climate change.

Feminist political geographers examine power. That is, they look at the effects of different kinds of power on the actions, decisions, attitudes, perceptions and experiences of different groups and individuals, from those who seem powerful, to those who seem relatively powerless. This includes obvious power relations as well as those often invisible ones that are embedded in social norms and privilege in the everyday life of dominant groups in society. When power is examined, it becomes evident that climate change is not an apolitical issue that can be simply fixed with better technology, more modelling, or simple behavioural adjustments. As climate justice activists point out, there are huge vested interests in maintaining the economic and social systems that maintain such privilege – namely capitalism and colonialism – that continue to drive climate change.

Yet in examining power, a feminist geography approach explores the points where inequality and unfairness can be challenged, alternatives envisioned and enacted and better, more care-filled communities can be developed. While this book describes the challenges of climate justice activism – from unfair media portrayals of 'dirty hippies', to police violence and surveillance, to burnout – we also point out the things that sustained activism and made it enjoyable for many people. Even though in many ways the economic and social drivers of climate change persist, there are incredibly hopeful shifts in the mainstreaming of climate change awareness, even climate justice, and there have been real shifts in policy settings in the past decade to reflect this.

As we write this, there are deep uncertainties about what lies ahead. Covid has been used to justify sweeping aside environmental protections to enable economic development, while health restrictions on public gatherings have prevented a lot of political organising (see PMC Editor 2020). For instance, in Canada the oil and gas industry was quick to argue for the relaxation of environmental protections and commitments to Indigenous rights because of the health and economic crisis (Indigenous Climate Action 2020). In West Virginia, a day after 'shelter in place' orders came into force, the governor signed into law an act that creates harsher penalties for anyone interfering with oil and gas infrastructure (Brown 2020). In July 2021, *The Guardian* reported on a recent analysis of how the US$17tn that has been put toward Covid-19 recovery stimulus packages has been spent. It found that only 10 per cent was dedicated to projects that would decrease global emissions or support conservation initiatives, putting into question any effort toward a 'green recovery' or reset (Harvey 2021).

In Aotearoa New Zealand, the early Covid response was praised for its success; borders were quickly closed, and the country went into a six-week lockdown through April and May 2020. There was a high degree of trust in the government and science communication about the virus that saw large public buy-in for the next twelve months. Covid was largely held at bay with only occasional outbreaks, mostly in Auckland through to late 2021 when more infectious strains emerged and strict containment measures no longer worked. During that initial phase until mid-2021, however, we also saw: the expansion of police powers, raising very real worries in Māori and Pasifika communities; extreme inequalities exposed through the very locations where outbreaks occurred; the vaccine roll-out and vaccine mandates that have divided communities;

a focus on big infrastructure-led economic recovery, with seemingly little regard for climate change in the decision-making process and outcome; an economic recovery that is amplifying inequality, and at the time nationalism and border worship. What does this nationalism in a time of crisis mean as the climate changes? What are the implications of widening inequality on our response to climate change? Our research doesn't directly answer these questions, but instead examines the nuances and subtle shifts of environmental campaigning and government and industry responses that changed the norms regulating the offshore environment in Aotearoa New Zealand. In exploring these shifts, we hope to highlight the spaces where pressure might be applied to shift communities towards climate justice.

THE REST OF THE BOOK

The story of the Oil Free campaign that we depict in this book is divided broadly into three parts. Chapters 2 and 3 set the scene. Aotearoa New Zealand, as a small island nation of 5 million people in the South Pacific, has a reputation as isolated and remote (maybe even sometimes backward), beautiful and 'pristine', punching above its weight in sports (especially in rugby and sometimes cricket), as a settler colony of Britain with a 'good' record compared to other states in terms of racial relations with Māori, and an economy largely based on tourism and agriculture (Bell 1996; Bond, Diprose and McGregor 2015; Byrnes 2006; Pawson 1997). However, the reality is different on a number of fronts. Aotearoa New Zealand has significant environmental concerns, with appalling records for biodiversity loss since the 1800s, significant habitat loss as a result of invasive species (flora and fauna), nationwide issues with water quality, and an emissions profile in which almost half of the country's gross greenhouse gas emissions are methane as a consequence of intensified agriculture. In addition, statistics for Māori health, incarceration rates, socio-economic status, as well as ongoing processes of land dispossession, and a government-led process of redress for colonial harm demonstrate the ongoing colonial processes that continue to oppress many Māori communities (Bargh 2007; Baxter et al. 2006; McIntosh and Workman 2013; Poata-Smith 2013; Ruckstuhl et al. 2014). Many of these issues have been exacerbated since the 1980s when Aotearoa New Zealand aggressively adopted neoliberalism becoming one of the most neoliberalised OECD countries. Our story starts here as the broader context in which the Oil Free campaign emerged.

In Chapter 2, we outline the tensions with Aotearoa New Zealand's neoliberal experiment which began with massive restructuring across all sectors in the 1980s. At the same time, a process of recognition of Te Tiriti o Waitangi[1] was also accelerating and taking shape after 150 years of struggle by Māori to demand that the government recognise what was promised in 1840. An English version of the Treaty was signed by the British Crown as a treaty of cession. But it was also translated into te reo (Māori language) and this version, signed by many Māori chiefs, had a very different meaning. This version guaranteed that Māori would retain their sovereignty over their lands (unceded), waters and taonga (treasured objects, valuable things). The period in the 1980s sets the context for the consolidation and extension of neoliberal approaches to global investment that resulted in Aotearoa New Zealand opening up the EEZ to the global petrochemical industry as well as ongoing negotiations around Treaty rights. From the mid-2000s that ultimately led to the events from which the Oil Free campaign emerged. In Chapter 3, we turn to the various events that heightened an awareness of the government's agenda for extraction at sea and how the campaign emerged and established itself into a network of grassroots groups across the country.

The second part of the book (Chapters 4–6) turns to the processes by which the campaign was undermined or as we term it, depoliticised, demonstrating the power of the petrochemical industry, investors, the media and sympathetic governments in securing their own interests. These chapters explore the various efforts to control, tame and delegitimise the message and various actions of the Oil Free activists. Again, situated within broader tendencies common within neoliberalised developed economies, the three chapters explore different tactics. In Chapter 4, we start with detailing the ways in which the media represented various actions that the different Oil Free groups engaged in, highlighting how the media consistently oriented readers and understandings of the issue toward a pragmatic realism on extraction, downplaying any environmental risk and promoting notions of economic gains. In addition, the media effectively delegitimised activists by emphasising sound bites from leading popular politicians and the oil and gas lobby. In turn, the chapter also outlines some activists' response to these delegitimisations by exploring how they framed their campaigns, drawing on eco-national identities prevalent in Aotearoa New Zealand and thereby downplaying their commitment to climate justice and drawing on 'average New Zealanders' to front actions.

Chapter 5 focuses on how different values were secured through the campaign, and the tactics and work that go into such securitisation by the oil and gas industry through promoting notions of corporate social responsibility and also enacting various surveillance practices. Through these tactics, the industry seeks to manage public perceptions and by trying to control the activities of the various Oil Free groups around the country. The chapter then explores the impact some of these practices had on individual activists.

The final chapter in this part of the book hones in on the third way in which attempts were made to depoliticise the Oil Free campaign. Chapter 6 turns to policing, situating the experiences of the activists we spoke to and their interactions with police in the context of policing in Western countries generally and in Aotearoa New Zealand more specifically. The chapter picks up on the ways in which racist social norms are reinforced through policing tactics, and how these interact with the historical trajectory of policing in the place where it occurs. It then turns to some specific examples our participants referred to, discussing violent encounters, experiences of dehumanisation and the police role in mediating whose rights to engage in lawful activities count most: protestors' right to non-violent action or the oil and gas industry in their exploration and drilling.

Representations of early actions in the media, as well as surveillance and policing, demonstrate the push-pull of activism, and also the particular moment in which the campaign was active. Even now at the time of writing, the media is significantly more sympathetic to climate justice arguments, perhaps influenced domestic activism and by international campaigns such as School Strike 4 Climate (as it's known in Aotearoa, more often called Fridays for Future elsewhere) and the actions of groups like Extinction Rebellion (XR). In addition, there is an indication of a slight shift in policing tactics in some places, where arrests and violence have been substituted for a more negotiated response, or arrests are followed by discharge with no conviction (Matthews 2021). This highlights the dynamic nature of any activist movement, and that it is also always situated in the local context, even though many characteristics are more generally translatable to experiences elsewhere.

The final part of the book comprises two chapters that turn to more hopeful encounters. Through thinking about hope, care and responsibility we focus on how activists engage in a care ethic that provides them both with the ability to collectively navigate the various tactics of delegitimisation and violence that is meted out to them in their work for a better world, while also highlighting how this ethic translates to a sense of responsibility that is assumed for climate injustices more generally. Here, we argue that the kind of care and responsibility articulated and practised by the climate justice activists in our study provide a counterpoint to the tactics of silencing and depoliticisation that are discussed in the preceding chapters. The ethic of care and responsibility that the activists we spoke to enact, subverts the ways in which neoliberalised practices more generally erode collective care and responsibility for humans and non-humans both in the local vicinity but also further afield, to the national and global levels. We pick up on this overall argument in the concluding chapter, drawing back to the wider context of climate justice, responsibility and action for change in the current neoliberalised global context.

2

Securing Oil

The story of the anti-deep-sea oil campaign begins with increased efforts to entice transnational petroleum corporations to explore Aotearoa's extensive EEZ. Aotearoa New Zealand was among the first countries to embrace wholesale neoliberal reforms in the 1980s, and this approach to governance, economic, social and environmental policy and practice has become embedded over subsequent decades. Understanding the historical trajectory in Aotearoa New Zealand is central to the period of climate change activism from 2008 to 2017 explored in subsequent chapters, because the governance in this period was a form of almost authoritarian neoliberalism that entrenched and consolidated an approach hailing Aotearoa New Zealand as 'open for business'.

Neoliberalism, a term more familiar to its critics, is a set of practices that pervasively shapes politics, economics and social relations across all scales from the global to the individual. It encapsulates the dominant form of economic and political practice globally, and has a set of foundational starting points and characteristics even though it manifests differently in different contexts. Core foundational tenets of neoliberalism are that the market is the best means to allocate resources; the state's role is to provide the means for the market to operate effectively; freedom refers to market freedom and individual freedom of choice; the market is adaptive and can therefore provide solutions by encouraging innovation and finally, that there is an emphasis on individual responsibility.

The origins of neoliberalism can be found in the 1920s and 1930s, with a small group of European intellectuals who were drawing on liberal ideas to counter socialism, and promote entrepreneurship and competition in the context of the Great Depression (Plehwe 2015). This marks the beginning of the intellectual genesis of neoliberalism. Interrupted by World War II, it wasn't until 1947 that these key individuals gathered at a conference in Mont-Pèlerin, Switzerland to develop their ideas, and formed the Mont Pèlerin Society (MPS). The MPS is a global network of intellectuals, largely independent of academic institutions, who developed the theoretical foundations of neoliberalism. But to suggest that the early years of the neoliberal 'thought collective' was (or has ever been) a singular unified movement would be wrong. It had diverse origins that were fragmented by the violent political and social context in Europe in the 1940s, which perhaps forced the group to be flexible and dynamic in response to changing conditions. Key economic principles however, were foundational, including the importance of a 'price mechanism' in market systems that shapes demand and supply of goods, free enterprise, competition, and a strong and impartial state. The movement was geographically spread across Europe, the US, and a range of other countries including Chile, Singapore, Australia and Aotearoa New Zealand. These diverse geographic locations were instrumental in the MPS eventually being able to put its theoretical ideas into practice in different countries.

The neoliberal thought collective put their theory into practice first in the 1970s and 1980s under leaders such as Margaret Thatcher in the UK, Ronald Reagan in the USA and Augusto Pinochet in Chile. This was enabled through the work of many actors in the global network of the MPS (Mirowski and Plehwe 2015; Peck 2010). Many of these actors held significant power and were able to influence government policy and initiatives at a time of economic and political flux in the late 1970s. For example, the think tanks such as the Institute of Economic Affairs in Britain and the Heritage Foundation in the US were well funded 'offshoots' of the MPS, and began to develop connections with academic institutions such as the Chicago School of Economics through MPS figures such as Milton Freidman (Peck 2010). As an influential educational institution, the Chicago School of Economics was significant in implementing the ideas of the MPS both generally and in governments across the globe. Nicknamed the Chicago Boys, a group of Chilean graduates from the Chicago school returned to Chile and influenced Pinochet's radical reforms, which took on a local flavour within the context of the violent military dictatorship. The global reach and influence of both the MPS and those affiliated was growing, enabling states to take up what they saw as an opportunity to experiment with radical reforms aimed at addressing significant economic issues. It was within this context in the 1980s that the 'New Zealand Experiment', as political theorist Jane Kelsey (1997) described it, began.

'THE NEW ZEALAND EXPERIMENT'

In the 1980s Aotearoa New Zealand undertook some of the fastest and most extensive neoliberal reforms across all sectors of society. The Minister of Finance in the fourth Labour Government, Roger Douglas, spearheaded the transformation, later dubbed 'Rogernomics'. Reforms in the 1980s included wholesale changes to the education sector by introducing 'user-pays' at tertiary level and a competitive funding model for schools, deregulating and removing subsidies in the agricultural sector, deregulating the financial sector, liberalising foreign exchange controls, changing monetary policy to focus on maintaining low inflation, privatising state assets, and cutting taxes for those in the top income brackets. Environmental regulation was significantly altered with the introduction of an entirely new resource management and urban planning regime. Consistent with the market-led orientation in this period, the regime is permissive of development providing environmental effects can be mitigated.

While the 1980s were known for Rogernomics, the 1990s were marked by 'Ruthanasia', a term given to the deepening of reforms begun in the 1980s but continued by the newly elected conservative National Party government's Finance Minister, Ruth Richardson. This resulted in further consolidation of neoliberalisation in the social sector. Means testing on welfare payments, the erosion of union power and the marketisation of labour, along with changes to state housing provision have also led to a steady increase in wealth disparities in recent decades. Key to the welfare reforms was the consolidation of a punitive discourse around the 'deserving' and 'undeserving' poor, and welfare benefits were significantly cut under Richardson's 'mother of all budgets' (as it has become known) in 1991. This first phase of neoliberalisation in the 1980s and 1990s reflects Peck and Tickell's (2002) description of 'roll-back' neoliberalism, whereby the state is rolled back and reduced in size and power with a view to the market assuming key functions, and the idea that in a liberalised economy, wealth will trickle down to those at the bottom end of the income hierarchy.

The second phase of neoliberalisation in Aotearoa New Zealand is evident from the late 1990s onward under a centre-left government, following a 'third way' approach to governance that reflected much of what was happening in the UK under New Labour. Here, neoliberalism is enabled to 'roll out' through the state providing mechanisms and support for markets to operate (Peck and Tickell 2002). In this period, neoliberal-isation was entrenched, though in less aggressive ways, and thereby also less controversially. Nevertheless, various aspects of this period provided the means for incentivising global investment in the petroleum industry, and facilitating exploration at sea by ensuring 'certainty' for investors, and low levels of environmental regulation.

A third phase of neoliberalisation is evident from 2008 to at least 2017 under a conservative government led by John Key, who was nicknamed on the left as the 'Teflon coated' 'smiling assassin'. Governance in this period can be associated with an erosion of core checks and balances in government (Geiringer et al. 2011; Thomas and Bond 2016), the use of 'dirty politics' to undermine democratic processes (Hager 2014), and a regime of austerity by stealth in the social sector (Baker and Davis 2018; Meese, Baker and Sisson 2020; Murphy 2020). The kind of authoritar-ian neoliberalism evident under Key's leadership paved the way for an agenda of policy initiatives oriented around incentivising overseas invest-ment in extractive industries by creating certainty for big business and an attractive economic and regulatory environment; by altering legis-lation through expedited processes that curtail parliamentary debate (Geiringer et al. 2011); and through an associated squeeze on democracy and activism (Bond, Diprose and Thomas 2019; see Chapter 3).

In 2008, John Key's government established what was described as a 'Business Growth Agenda', which included the sale of state assets, and the development of extractive industries. The orientation toward extractive industries was demonstrated through media that referred to an increasing need to catch up with Australia, and government ministers comment-ing on the need to make the 'most use of the wealth hidden in our hills, under the ground and in our oceans' (Hekia Parata, quoted in Kay 2011). These comments suggest that it is possible to engage in resource extrac-tive activities responsibly, and at the same time, it is the morally right thing to do to maintain lifestyles and economic growth in the twenty-first century. Various initiatives followed, some of which were strongly con-tested, demonstrating the degree to which the government was limited in progressing the agenda. For example, a stocktake of mineral wealth was undertaken on land in the conservation estate (National Parks and other protected areas), which comprise about a third of the country. Following from the stocktake, the government then sought to remove clauses from legislation that banned mining from 7,000 ha of the most ecologically and scenically valuable parts of the conservation estate, including National

Parks (Bond, Diprose and McGregor 2015). The outcry from the public was loud and persistent, voiced through the 2Precious2Mine campaign led by international environmental groups like Greenpeace, but taken up across the country through petitions and protests. In 2010, conservative estimates say 20,000 people marched down Auckland's busy Queen Street, while others say it was more like 50,000 people (Bond, Diprose and McGregor 2015). Similar marches occurred across the country. In addition, the proposed legislative change received 37,552 submissions, of which 98 per cent were opposed to the removal of the protections (Ministry of Business, Innovation and Employment n.d.). This is significant for a country with a population of only 4.5 million at the time. Ultimately, the government withdrew the proposal later that year, but the issue heightened awareness of the risks of extractive industries as well as providing a reminder of the power of widespread protest.

Another key part of the Business Growth Agenda was a series of initiatives that actively sought to attract international investment in the oil and gas sector within Aotearoa New Zealand's EEZ. The EEZ is an area over which a nation-state has partial sovereignty, including to extract resources, demarcated under the United Nations Convention of the Law of the Sea. It extends to approximately 200 nautical miles from the coastline. Given its maritime nature, Aotearoa New Zealand's EEZ is extensive, spanning some three million square kilometres. It is 15 times the land area of Aotearoa and the fifth largest in the world. The New Zealand government's intention was consistent with international trends and 'blue frontier' narratives (Zalik 2018), in which ocean spaces are represented as the last frontiers to be explored, discovered, and exploited.

In the context of petroleum resources, 'cheap' oil – that which is accessible and easy to extract – has become more scarce. However, as technology has improved, the industry has turned to more remote areas such as the 'blue frontier' (Kristoffersen and Young 2010) in its search for black gold. The then government's approach to attracting investors in order to 'make use' of such an extensive resource, included establishing a tender process, called a 'block offer' for permits to explore for petroleum resources across significant parts of the EEZ, in order to 'maximise the gains from the responsible development of our oil and gas resources' (Action 1 of 8 in the 2009 Petroleum Action Plan). A significantly increased area of the EEZ was offered for tender in the period from 2008 to 2016. Within this context the Brazilian oil company, Petrobras, took up one such permit in 2010, and became embroiled in a conflict with local iwi (Māori tribe) Te

Whānau-ā-Apanui. This conflict marked the emergence of the Oil Free campaign and may have resulted in the Anadarko Amendment, referred to in the introductory chapter. Both of these events are discussed further in Chapter 3. Four decades on from the initial neoliberal experiment, Aotearoa New Zealand remains among the most 'neoliberalised' (Kelsey 2015). But as forms of neoliberalism shift within the context of global drivers such as the global financial crisis of 2008, and at the time of writing the global Covid-19 pandemic, it is also always localised in the practices, policies and politics of nation-states and regions. And so, some further context on the role of Māori, Te Tiriti o Waitangi and petroleum resources is required.

TE TIRITI O WAITANGI

At the same time as the drastic and far-reaching neoliberal reforms in the 1980s described above, Aotearoa New Zealand also embarked on a process of formalised redress for Māori under Te Tiriti o Waitangi. The neoliberalisation of Aotearoa New Zealand was therefore inflected by significant simultaneous shifts in Indigenous–Crown (or government) relations. These shifts centred around the long overdue legal recognition of the Treaty in 1975.

Te Tiriti o Waitangi was signed in 1840 between the representatives of the British Crown, and some iwi (or tribal) chiefs across Aotearoa. As noted in Chapter 1, there are two versions of the Treaty with very different meanings embedded in them. The English language version of the document (referred to in the following as the Treaty of Waitangi) clearly states that Māori cede sovereignty to the Crown and it is a treaty of cession, in exchange for the Crown's protection of Māori as British subjects. However, the version in te reo, the Māori language (referred to in the following as Te Tiriti o Waitangi), is the version signed by most Māori chiefs, and does not cede sovereignty. Indeed, the likely interpretation of the te reo text at the time was that the Queen would control the lawlessness of Pākehā (white New Zealanders) through 'kāwanatanga' (a transliteration of governance) while Māori were promised rangatiratanga (akin to sovereignty but much more far reaching, see Fitzmaurice and Bargh 2022) over their lands, forests and treasures (Mutu 2010). For Māori, as for other Indigenous groups subject to similar Treaty negotiations in the eighteenth and nineteenth centuries, the English version of the Treaty makes no sense, for to cede sovereignty over the land would be to surrender the identity of being Māori, or tangata whenua, people of the land. In addition, international law favours the Indigenous language version when there are substantive differences, such as in this case. As a result, the Treaty of Waitangi (English text) and Te Tiriti o Waitangi (te reo text) are two treaties, and for Māori in particular, it was Te Tiriti (not the English version) that was agreed to and provides certain promises and obligations on the part of the Crown, represented by the New Zealand government.

Throughout this book, we write about 'Te Tiriti o Waitangi' as the founding document and the 1840 text that has international legal standing. We write about 'The Treaty/Te Tiriti' referring to the sometimes ambiguous ways both documents signed in the 1840s are invoked, for instance in public and official discourse where sometimes te reo text is implied, and at other times it implies something more palatable to the Crown. We write about 'The Treaty' when that reflects the language used in legislation for example. Our shifting language reflects wider discourses and the ongoing struggles between colonialism, decolonisation and the restoration of tino rangatiratanga.

Struggles for recognition of the promises made in Te Tiriti (the te reo version) have been ongoing, and have often been met with violence. In the last 40 years, there have been some gains. The 1970s marked a period of significant and much more visible mobilisation by Māori demanding recognition of continuing breaches of Te Tiriti, oppression and marginalisation of Māori through violent assimilationist policies, and the demand that 'not one more acre' of Māori land be lost. The Treaty of Waitangi Act 1975 was one parliamentary response to decades of persistent mobilisation by Māori, and came at a time when Indigenous movements were coming to prominence around the world.

The Act provided a mechanism, through the establishment of the Waitangi Tribunal, through which Māori could claim that the 'principles' of the Treaty of Waitangi had been breached. Use of phrase 'principles of the Treaty of Waitangi' was, at the time of legislating, a middle ground to reflect the divergence between the two language versions of the Treaty. Much legislation, until recently, has also incorporated a directive that decisions must 'recognise', 'take account of' or 'have regard' to the 'principles of the Treaty of Waitangi'. Although the Treaty/Te Tiriti is regarded as the founding constitutional document by the government, the role of the Waitangi Tribunal and the courts in determining what the 'principles' are has been highly contested. The principles of the Treaty/Te Tiriti are derived from a combination of sources including the two texts – the Treaty and Te Tiriti, the intentions and cultural meanings that both Māori and the Crown would have given to the words, and legal interpretation practices. The current government has endorsed an approach to interpreting the Treaty/Te Tiriti that was established in the 1990s whereby the Treaty is considered as a whole, including its 'underlying meaning, intention and spirit' and as a living document that will evolve as times change (Hancock and Gover 2001, p. 77; Hayward 2015). This is supported by some Māori, the courts and the Waitangi Tribunal. A general set of principles have been established through this approach, including:

- partnership between Māori and the Crown which infers that both the Crown and Māori act reasonably and in good faith;
- the active protection of Māori and their interests by the Crown;
- various articulations of reciprocity whereby the Crown is given the right to govern in exchange for Māori rights to retain their tribal authority, control over themselves and their interests, and a right to development; and
- a duty to consult Māori on matters affecting their interests (see Hayward 2015).

However, this relatively flexible interpretive approach to Treaty principles has also frustrated many others. For some Māori, adopting 'principles' enables the Crown to continue various forms of colonialism, and continue to breach what was actually promised in Te Tiriti. That is, it allows the Crown to seek a 'balance' between the two versions of the Treaty, rather than fulfil the promise of rangatiratanga or full chieftainship and absolute authority. In contrast, some Pākehā (white New Zealanders) seem to prefer either specific statements that give effect to the clauses of the Treaty/Te Tiriti, or that clauses referring to the principles are definitively fixed, providing greater certainty in their application. The adaptability of the principles of the Treaty/Te Tiriti is a double-edged sword. On one hand, it provides the means to interpret Te Tiriti in a way that is culturally appropriate for Māori as well as being able to adapt to changing social, political, environmental and development conditions over time (Hamer 2015). On the other, it also provides the opportunity for the achievements Māori have gained in the last 45 years in securing some recognition of partnership and associated Crown obligations to be eroded. As discussed further below, more recent legislation has adopted a more prescriptive approach to incorporating the obligations laid out in Te Tiriti into law, demonstrating the ongoing contestation surrounding responsibilities and duties established in 1840.

The mechanism for inquiring into breaches of Treaty principles that was established under the Waitangi Act is through a commission of inquiry called the Waitangi Tribunal. Although the Tribunal had a somewhat faltering start and was at risk of being characterised as a tokenistic gesture, adopting inappropriate Western processes, it gradually gained momentum after a well-respected Māori Land Court judge, Edward Taihakurei Durie became chair in 1980, and adapted the processes to incorporate a more Māori approach to hearings (Hamer 2015). In 1985 an amendment to the Act enabled claims to be made for past breaches, dating back to 1840 when the Treaty/Te Tiriti was signed. However, and as noted at the beginning of this section, the Tribunal was established in the:

> midst of a collision between two contradictory forces: on the one hand, a genuine political will to improve the situation for Māori; on the other, a new commitment to neo-liberal economic policies that transformed state structures and undermined the capacity to fulfil the promise generated by that political will. (Joseph 2000, cited in Bargh 2007, p. 28)

Bargh (2007) argues that at the time of establishment, the Tribunal was not expected to receive many claims, meet often, nor cost very much and was an attempt at placation. Yet it has become a crucial way for Māori to draw attention to grievances, seek redress for past and present breaches of Te Tiriti, and gain recognition for the past and ongoing violence of colonisation. Despite the Tribunal's slow start, by 1991, 200 claims had been lodged, swelling to 600 by 1996. The Tribunal is still under-resourced, demonstrated by the continuous backlog of claims (Hamer 2015). Claims made to the Tribunal by Māori are researched and heard adopting Māori cultural practices and protocols throughout. A comprehensive report documents findings and recommendations and if the claim is verified as a breach, the recommendations are formally put to the government for redress. If the government decides the claim is valid, it engages in negotiation to reach a settlement for reparation and compensation. Since the early 1990s almost 75 iwi (Māori tribal groups) have settled historic claims of significant breaches for lost land and taonga. At the time of writing, about half a dozen groups are in some stage of negotiation with the Crown, and some iwi are still to settle their most significant land claims.[1] However, the Tribunal also hears claims that go beyond land loss, including rights and access to resources, such as petroleum.

MINERALS AND PETROLEUM

Māori cosmologies include various references to oil and gas through legends that refer to specific landforms' relationships to minerals and atua (deities, ancestors, gods), or seepages as tapu (sacred, a supernatural state) (Waitangi Tribunal 2003). Hapū (kinship group, clan, subtribe) and iwi have specific relationships with petroleum as part of a genealogical connection (whakapapa) with the natural world. Colonial records also observed oil and gas seepages in both Taranaki and areas of the east coast of the North Island in the 1800s. Early Pākehā attempts to extract oil from locations where there was obvious seepage at the land surface were noted in Taranaki from 1865 (Waitangi Tribunal 2003). Despite recognition of the value of oil and various efforts at extraction, it wasn't until 1906 that technology allowed for commercial extraction by the Taranaki Petroleum Company at Moturoa. An early boom followed prior to World War I, but limited technology and the absence of a local refinery meant that demand and production remained low and localised. Exploration continued, but sustained production did not become established until the 1970s, when the Kapuni field was discovered and became commercially productive (Waitangi Tribunal 2003).

Legislation – the Crown Minerals Act 1991 – dictates that the Crown owns all gold, silver, uranium and petroleum in Aotearoa New Zealand. Such legislation is common in colonial countries following the Westminster style of government. Through colonisation, British law was extended to Aotearoa New Zealand, violently displacing the Māori legal system or tikanga, based on a world view and values in which past, present and future relationships between people and between people and things are central to identity (Ruru 2018). Under British law, all resources (except gold and silver) on the surface of land and under it belonged to the owner of that land (MBIE 2011; Waitangi Tribunal 2003; NZPAM 2013). The exception for gold and silver, known as the Royal Prerogative and dating back to the 1500s, was extended to include other precious minerals as their value became apparent. In 1937, the Petroleum Act extinguished all private ownership of petroleum resources, reserving the resource for the

Crown (Waitangi Tribunal 2003). Crown ownership enabled the government to control all extraction, even when located in private land, and take royalties. The Crown Minerals Act 1991 is the contemporary legislation that regulates exploration and extraction activities of these Crown-owned minerals. The Act works in combination with other legislation that manages activities and planning on land and at sea.

In 1999, the ownership of petroleum resources was formally questioned by Māori in a claim to the Waitangi Tribunal. They argued that Te Tiriti protected proprietary rights to resources in their territories, including oil and gas (Ruckstahl et al. 2014; Waitangi Tribunal 2003). The claim (Wai 796) was urgently taken to the Waitangi tribunal in 2000 as the government sought to sell its interests in the Kupe oil field off the Taranaki coast. The claim was heard in two parts, the first reflecting the urgency required because of the government's pending decision at the time, while the second part took more time to consider broader issues associated with managing the resource. The result was two reports of the Tribunal for the Wai 796 claim, one released in 2003 on the status of the resource itself, and one released in 2011 on the governance and management regime of petroleum.

PETROLEUM CLAIMS IN THE WAITANGI TRIBUNAL

In the first report of the Wai 796 claim released in 2003, Māori argued that the 'extinguishment' of the possession of petroleum as a taonga or treasure through the 1937 Act was a breach of Te Tiriti. At the time the Act was passed, Māori objected on the basis that they would lose all rights to petroleum, not necessarily as a resource but as part of the land that ought to have been protected under the Treaty (see also Ruckstuhl et al. 2014). The claims before the Waitangi Tribunal explored the process by which the 1937 Act came into force, and the parliamentary debates at the time which focused on whether sufficient account was taken of Māori interests, particularly in relation to whether royalties should be paid to Māori. The arguments from 1937 documented in the report reflect those often made today – that Pākehā and Māori should be treated equally under one law; that the very thought of having to pay royalties to Māori would be a disincentive for investors; and that all opportunities to develop such a vital resource should be taken. These points demonstrate the perception in the 1930s of the necessity to secure control over petroleum, and the early recognition of the value of the resource. For example, the report notes a comment by the then Under-Secretary of the Mines Department, that:

> the importance of petroleum and its products is now so great in both our national and Empire economy and also has such a tremendous bearing on the question of defence, that it should be obvious that no opportunity should be lost in attempting to develop a local oil industry. (Waitangi Tribunal 2003, p. 28)

Documents reveal explicit recognition that the 1937 Act would be 'contrary to the "spirit and letter" of the Treaty', but securing the resource was deemed a 'matter of national importance' that warranted not observing the Treaty 'to the full' (Waitangi Tribunal 2003, p. 28). The ultimate justification for passing the Act was that it treated Pākehā and Māori equally, and equated the 'spirit and letter of the Treaty' with a simple duty not to discriminate. This was challenged at the time without success.

In 2003, the Tribunal found that while the nationalisation of petroleum was an important step in securing a resource, the way the nationalisation excluded prior owners of the resource from royalties was unjustified and a breach of article 2 of the Treaty, that guarantees Māori possession and sovereignty over their taonga. The 1937 Act and subsequent decisions under the 1991 Act breach the Treaty principle that requires the Crown to actively protect Māori interests. As a consequence, the Tribunal argues that the breach gives rise to a 'Treaty interest' in the petroleum resource, which implies a right to remedy and redress. The interest in petroleum resources that Māori, according to the Tribunal, should have maintained means that Māori should have the right to determine whether or not to extract. In turn this means that there is a central role for Māori within the governance and management of the resource as an exercise of their sovereignty as guaranteed by Te Tiriti.

Indeed, this was discussed further in the second part of the claim, that was not reported on until 2011 (Waitangi Tribunal 2011). Here, the Tribunal examined the legislative, regulatory and management regime of oil and gas exploration and mining both onshore and offshore for its consistency with the principles of the Treaty of Waitangi. They found it wanting in a number of respects. Although the Crown argued that there is a 'culture of consultation', Māori claim that this often does not occur in practice. The Tribunal found three key systemic flaws in the regulatory regime that support the Māori claim. First, Māori do not have the capacity (primarily time and resources) to participate in the processes of the legislative regime. Second, there is little or no monitoring of local authorities' actions in terms of their obligations under the Treaty, and so there is no way of assessing the degree to which this consultation culture actually meets Treaty principles. In particular, there is insufficient recognition of te ao Māori (the Māori world and ways of doing things) within the regulatory regime and by local authorities in particular. The Tribunal argues that these are Crown failings as the responsibilities under the various statutes are delegated by the Crown to local authorities. And third, as a consequence of the first two flaws, Māori values, perspectives and interests are not sufficiently accounted for in decision-making on petroleum exploration and extraction.

While the Tribunal recognises that the management and regulation of oil and gas is complex with a range of different interests, Māori are more than just another stakeholder or interest group, and there are a number of prejudices that limit Māori in effectively taking up opportunities to engage. The Tribunal reported that:

> Māori feel powerless where they ought to be partners. The effect is that Māori cannot exercise kaitiakitanga[2] to protect and conserve for future generations the taonga with which they have been entrusted. Instead, they must watch as their sacred sites are 'modified', interfered with, or simply obliterated. They have been reduced to the role of submitters in a long line of interested and potentially affected parties. Largely lacking in adequate resources to properly engage with the decision-makers, their frustrations were readily apparent in the evidence. Over time, the capability of the claimants to protect their lands and other taonga has been significantly undermined. (Waitangi Tribunal 2011, p. 165)

The Tribunal claimants' demand for a more effective role within the petroleum regime is further strengthened by the UN Declaration on the Rights of Indigenous People (UNDRIP 2007), to which Aotearoa New Zealand is a signatory. The UNDRIP requires that full prior informed consent on developments and projects that affect Indigenous interests is given by those Indigenous groups. Despite the Tribunal's recommendations and the obligations under UNDRIP, changes to the Crown Minerals Act in 2013 failed to make consultation with Māori mandatory. Instead, the changes established a system whereby petroleum companies report on their engagement with iwi and hapū annually. As discussed further in

Chapter 3, the social licence for transnational petrochemical companies to operate in Aotearoa New Zealand involves meeting both Te Tiriti and UNDRIP obligations (Ruckstuhl et al. 2014). The soft approach to consultation fails to meet those obligations. Opportunities to strengthen the duty to consult, let alone build partnership, under Te Tiriti and UNDRIP were also ignored when legislation governing extractive industries in the EEZ was enacted in 2012.

Prior to 2012, there were a number of instances where the absence of regulations over the ocean spaces of the EEZ was highlighted, including in the 2011 Waitangi Report on Petroleum discussed above. New legislation was introduced in 2012 called the Exclusive Economic Zone and Continental Shelf (Environmental Effects) Act (referred to here as the EEZ Act). This legislation provides for a regulatory regime for the EEZ that parallels the primary planning and resource management legislation on land. It requires marine consents for any activity proposed in the EEZ that is not specifically 'permitted', and provides mechanisms for making decisions about consents. The Act fills a necessary gap in resource regulation for activities at sea that may have significant environmental effects, but there has been some concern that it does not go far enough in some respects. Specifically, the legislation was an opportunity to strengthen provisions in relation to Māori roles in decision-making in response to the Wai 796 claim and recommendations. However, the Act does the opposite and highlights the ongoing tensions around the interpretation of 'Treaty principles'.

As noted above, since the 1980s and 1990s legislation has explicitly incorporated the phrase, 'principles of the Treaty of Waitangi' in their wording. At the time this was significant because it was the first legal recognition of Te Tiriti. The original reference to 'principles' in the Treaty of Waitangi Act 1975 was a means to navigate a middle path between the two texts of the Treaty rather than favouring the Indigenous language text as is common practice in international law. Phrases such as 'take account of' or 'have regard to' or even 'give effect to' the 'principles of the Treaty of Waitangi' became a feature in key environmental legislation. Despite the middle path the use of the term 'principles' took (rather than adopting the te reo text), this period marked significant gains in recognising the Treaty in resource management law. In the late 1980s and early 1990s the courts and Waitangi Tribunal had a significant role in determining what those principles are, and understandings of the principles are now well established. However, the Crown, legislators, and others have more recently sought to narrow these understandings, arguing that it puts too much power into the hands of the courts, is too uncertain, and has the potential to result in too much litigation, or 'judicial review' – the process of taking decision-makers to court if they have applied the law incorrectly in their decision-making. Consequently, there has been a shift away from such terminology, which is reflected in the EEZ Act.

Instead of a specific requirement for decision-makers under the EEZ Act to take account of, or give effect to Treaty principles, the Act contains a section that declares *how* and in which sections the Act meets Treaty obligations (e.g. Section 12). These include establishing a Māori Advisory Board within the regulating agency, providing an opportunity for Māori to be consulted when regulations that provide decision-making criteria are drafted, a requirement to consider affected interests, and to 'notify' iwi affected by any developments in the EEZ. Submissions on the Bill as it went through Parliament showed concern at this shift in legislative practice, specifically the way in which it narrowed the Treaty to a form of consultation (i.e. being only 'notified') that does not reflect the principles of partnership let alone the stipulation that full prior informed consent be sought from affected Indigenous Peoples as stated in the UNDRIP.[3] The way the Treaty is incorporated in the EEZ Act narrows the grounds for Māori to raise questions about decision-making processes that might breach Te Tiriti because the legislation itself determines what aspects of the principles are relevant. In the past, this has not been the role of legislators, but has been undertaken by the Waitangi Tribunal and courts, in order to recognise the spirit of Te Tiriti and the context in which it was signed, to apply a te ao Māori interpretation and as a result of the Treaty's character as a living document (Hamer 2015). We argue that the more prescriptive approach to legislation demonstrated in the EEZ Act is a step even further away from Te Tiriti than the original middle path taken in adopting the terminology around 'principles'. This legislative approach and the limitations on iwi involvement in deciding whether, where and how petroleum extraction occurs suggest a fear of Māori sovereignty, compromising the governments control over the resource. Rather, a Te Tiriti response would recognise the role of iwi sovereignty.

The principles of the Treaty of Waitangi established that the cornerstone of the Treaty of Waitangi is that Māori and the Crown are in partnership, with obligations to act in good faith and to protect Māori interests (Hayward 2019). In relation to oil and gas exploration and extraction, and consistent with the findings of the Waitangi Tribunal, affected iwi should have a far greater role than simply to be notified when the oil and gas industry deem that their activities involve iwi rohe moana (territories at sea), or to be invited to comment on regulations made under the Act.

CONCLUSION

This chapter has set out the broader geopolitical-economic context, including neoliberalisations and Treaty relations within Aotearoa New Zealand. These characteristics are common to many other places that have embraced neoliberalism. However, as we have highlighted, they also demonstrate the adaptive nature of neoliberalism to the specific places in which it manifests. The first two sections of the chapter characterised the nature and dominance of neoliberalisations that have occurred in Aotearoa since the 1980s. This time period marked a major transformation in the primary ideology shaping governance processes, systems and decision-making across all sectors. This period also coincided with the increasing recognition of the bicultural character of Aotearoa New Zealand through much more meaningful recognition of Te Tiriti o Waitangi and the development of a system of redress for past and ongoing breaches of Aotearoa's founding agreement between Māori and the Crown. The specific role of the petroleum sector in this context was also explored, highlighting ongoing tensions around the nature of Māori involvement in decision-making when a resource is as highly valued as oil. These tensions – between efforts by the state to secure control, management and development of the resource on one hand, and Māori sovereignty and whakapapa (genealogical) entanglements with taonga and the natural world on the other – is central to the emergence of the Oil Free campaign, introduced in the Chapter 3.

3

Contesting Oil

The Aotearoa New Zealand government's agenda for the oil and gas sector described in its Business Growth Agenda of 2008 (see Chapter 2) didn't go unnoticed by climate justice and environmental activists nor iwi groups, many of whom were already active against coal mining. What differed perhaps was an increased sensitisation to oil and gas exploration at sea amongst the wider public. A number of events were responsible for this growing awareness. In Chapter 2 we noted the 2010 campaign, 2Precious2Mine, against mining in the conservation estate that emerged as a direct result of the government's short-lived attempt to remove legal protections that prohibits it (Bond, Diprose and McGregor 2015). Other events sensitised the Aotearoa New Zealand public to the risks of oil and gas drilling at sea.

Globally, the Deep Water Horizon spill in the Gulf of Mexico highlighted the dangers of drilling in deep water ocean environments. In April 2010, an explosion at the wellhead of the Deep Water Horizon drilling platform resulted in an oil spill of 210 million gallons of crude oil which is estimated to have spread over 149,000 kilometres. Various factors, including the depth and pressure of the spill meant that it took a full 87 days to cap. At the time of writing, it is recognised as the largest oil spill from a single source at sea. The implications of the spill, and the extent of damage caused, were still being identified a decade after the event (The Maritime Executive 2020). In addition, the climate movement had gained considerable momentum just prior to COP15 in Copenhagen. Although the meeting failed to agree to the kinds of targets demanded by the movement (Vidal, Stratton and Goldenberg 2009), a proliferation of activist and grassroots groups gathered in the city to protest following what has been described as an 'upsurge' in climate activism in the late 2000s (Rosewarne, Goodman and Pearse 2013).

In Aotearoa New Zealand, as the government sought to deliver on its Business Growth Agenda, two further events sensitised the public to the risks of engaging in extractive industry in ocean environments and the power of corporates to elude their responsibilities. First, the *Rena* disaster occurred in Tauranga, off the east coast of the North Island. The *Rena* was a container ship that ran aground on the Ōtāiti/Astrolabe reef in October 2011 while on its way into Tauranga Harbour. The ship broke up over a period of months, leaving fuel and debris from containers littered across the ocean and local beaches. As the costs of managing the disaster escalated, the inadequacy of environmental regulation and the inability to force international corporates to take financial responsibility for such accidents were highlighted. The *Rena* was flagged to Liberia, but chartered to the Mediterranean Shipping Company. Maritime law only required the shipping company to pay a maximum of NZ$11.3 million in compensation for losses that resulted from the accident (Waitangi Tribunal 2015). While further payments were negotiated between the government, the shipping company and insurers, some estimate the cost of the clean-up has reached NZ$660 million, still excluding removal of the wreck, half of which remains on the reef (Schiel, Ross and Battershill 2016).

These events also demonstrate the ongoing invisibilisation of Māori relationships with ocean spaces. As resource consent applications to leave the partial wreck on the reef were heard, local Māori lodged two urgent claims to the Waitangi Tribunal (Waitangi Tribunal 2015). Ōtāiti, the reef where half of the Rena continues to lie, and nearby Mōtītī Island are tipua, or uncanny spiritual things to the people of Mōtītī (Evans 2016; Waitangi Tribunal 2015). Claimants to the Waitangi Tribunal argued that the reef forms the 'stepping stones for the wairua [spirit] of our deceased' (Waitangi Tribunal 2015, p. 14). In turn, Māori have specific obligations in being kaitiaki, or guardians, of these tipua and taonga (treasured things). The grounding of the Rena and subsequent clean up, including the risk of further contamination from the partial wreck that remains on the reef, has both a 'physical and a metaphysical impact on affected iwi [tribal groups]' (Evans 2016, p. 3). The Waitangi Tribunal found that Treaty principles had been breached in terms of inadequate consultation during the resource consent hearings and a failure to actively protect Māori taonga.

While subsequent legislation substantially increased the amount payable by shipping companies in such situations (New Zealand Government 2012), there is still inadequate acknowledgement of Māori taonga and the Crown's obligations to actively protect them to give meaning to a Treaty partnership in environmental legislation.

The second event that sensitised the public to the risks of offshore extraction occurred at the beginning of 2011, a couple of months earlier than the *Rena* disaster, and was directly related to oil and gas exploration at sea. It was a direct precursor to the emergence of the oil free campaign across Aotearoa New Zealand.

THE EMERGENCE OF DISSENT

On the east coast of the North Island of Aotearoa New Zealand, a small iwi or tribal group, Te Whānau-ā-Apanui, with support from Greenpeace New Zealand, disrupted a large Brazilian petroleum company, Petrobras, from their seismic surveying of the Raukūmara Basin, in the EEZ. Petrobras had secured a five-year permit to explore for oil and gas under block offers released in 2010. Some efforts to consult with Te Whānau-ā-Apanui were made by the Ministry of Energy prior to the block offers being released, and Te Whānau-ā-Apanui had requested that no exploration for oil and gas be undertaken in their area. They also indicated that they were unable to engage in full consultation at that time, as other pressing regulatory changes affecting their rohe (or territory) were in process (Erueti and Pietras 2013). Once Petrobras had secured their permit, they met with local iwi and community groups on several occasions. Te Whānau-ā-Apanui consistently indicated that they would not provide consent for the seismic surveying work or any future oil and gas production, due to concerns about the effects of these activities on marine ecology and the importance of their fisheries (see Forney et al. 2017). Nevertheless, Petrobras informed Te Whānau-ā-Apanui that they would begin their seismic survey work in early 2011, and began work in April using the large survey vessel, the *Orient Explorer*.

Opposition to Petrobras began quickly both onshore and offshore, demanding 'no drill, no spill'. The impacts of the Deep Water Horizon spill in the Gulf of Mexico were still fresh news, particularly given that the blow-out occurred at a depth of 1500 m, and the significant difficulty of capping the exploded wellhead even at that (relatively shallow) depth. The marine response to the Deep Water Horizon spill was of a scale and resource that would be impossible to pull together in Aotearoa New Zealand in a timely fashion, and much of the Raukūmara Basin is at 3,000 m depth. These safety concerns combined with those of Te Whānau-ā-Apanui, particularly in relation to their Indigenous rights under Te Tiriti, the UNDRIP and the impacts of climate change from oil and gas drilling were the primary motivations for action. Offshore, a flotilla of five vessels sailed out to the seismic survey vessel to attempt to halt its work over a period of seven weeks, where actions included sailing and swimming in front of the survey vessel (Erueti and Peitras 2013). Rikirangi Gage, a tribal leader, provides a clear indication of the iwi's position in his radio call to the *Orient Explorer*. He stated:

You are not welcome in our waters. Accordingly and as an expression of our mana [authority, jurisdiction] in these waters and our deep concern for the adverse effects of deep sea drilling, we will be positioning the Te Whānau-ā-Apanui vessel directly in your path, approximately one and a half nautical miles in front of you.

We will not be moving, we will be doing some fishing. We wish to reiterate that this is not a protest. We are defending tribal waters and our rights from reckless Government policies and the threat of deep sea drilling, which our hapū [group within an iwi or tribe] have not consented to and continue to oppose. We have a duty to uphold the mana of our hapū here in our territorial waters. (Peace Movement Aotearoa 2011)

This statement represents the iwi's claim to rangatiratanga over their waters. The statement contests the development agenda the government adopted, extraction of oil and gas in their rohe moana, and opposes the regulatory framework that prioritises economic interests and overseas investment in the petroleum industry. It also situates their position in relation to upholding Te Tiriti o Waitangi.

Petrobras complained to the Ministry of Energy, and also warned that they would withdraw if community action continued (Hill 2011). There was also much discussion in the media and online at this time, questioning how the actions of the protestors could be managed, given the lack of a legislative regime in the EEZ, where the protest occurred. Following advice from the Ministry of Justice, on 23 April the New Zealand Navy was used to transport police to the flotilla, and rather dramatically, arrest the skipper of the *San Pietro*, a fishing vessel owned by Te Whānau-ā-Apanui (Peace Movement Aotearoa 2011). Images in the media portrayed a 'David and Goliath' scene as the small fishing boat was dwarfed against the metallic grey of the massive Navy vessels. In December 2012, Petrobras withdrew from the area, stating that there was insufficient petroleum to warrant further exploration (Bradley 2012). In contrast, Te Whānau-ā-Apanui claimed that a key reason Petrobras' withdrew was that the protest actions shifted the financial equation and made the investment too expensive and risky, exposed gaps in the regulatory regime and created too much uncertainty for the corporation (Takitimu 2016).

CLOSING DOWN SPACE FOR DISSENT

Following these events, a number of meetings were reportedly held between government agencies and industry representatives concerned by the lack of a regulatory regime in the EEZ and the risk of protesters disrupting lawful permitted activities (*New Zealand Herald* 2013). Not long after these discussions, two significant legislative changes were made that affected the way in which protestors and the public might express their views on whether and where oil and gas drilling and exploration can occur. The first was the enactment of the EEZ Act 2012, referred to in Chapter 2. As noted, there was clearly a need for some form of management regime for environmental protection. However, given the context in which it was drafted, we suggest it was also intended to provide certainty to investors with operations in the EEZ (Ministry for the Environment 2011). Part of this certainty is provided through an explicit effort to limit the opportunity for the public to be involved in decisions on exploration consents (Ministry for the Environment n.d.; Somerville, Paine and Tripp 2014). The only requirement under the Act is for affected iwi to be notified. As discussed above, this is a particularly weak interpretation of Treaty obligations. The Act provides no requirement for formal consultation, let alone 'free, prior and informed consent' as required under the United Nations Declaration on the Rights of Indigenous Peoples to which Aotearoa New Zealand is a signatory. In addition, regulations under the Act mean that oil and gas exploration permits are processed on a 'non-notified' basis. This means that they are not notified to the public and there is no process by which the public can comment on them through formal submissions (as would be the case had they been notified). The Ministry for the Environment claimed, as the EEZ Bill went through Parliament, that 'the value of effective public participation in decision-making cannot be "quantified", while the savings to industry can' (Ministry for the Environment, n.d.). So while the purpose of the EEZ Act is to provide for the sustainable management of the EEZ, it has inadequate provisions relating to Te Tiriti o Waitangi and public consultation. It appears to be a regulatory instrument that is relatively pro-development, designed to provide certainty to investors in the petroleum sector by minimising the potential for dissent. This is consistent with the overall agenda of the government at the time, the orientation toward increasing the economic benefits of extractive industries and the close relationships between the government and industry (see Chapter 5).

The second piece of legislation that was enacted in this timeframe after the flotilla and actions of Te Whānau-ā-Apanui and Greenpeace in the Raukūmara Basin, was an amendment to the Crown Minerals Act 1991 mentioned in Chapter 1. This amendment criminalised protest at sea near a vessel engaged in petroleum exploration or drilling. When the captain of the Te Whānau-ā-Apanui vessel, the *San Pietro* was arrested by police for obstructing the Petrobras vessel's seismic survey (discussed above), there was some debate in the media on what charges could be laid against the protestors. In the end, the Maritime Transport Act 1994 was used, and the skipper, Elvis Teddy, was charged with a 'blatant breach of safety' (Hill 2011). The appropriateness of this choice was contested in court later in terms of whether or not the application of the Act extended beyond the territorial sea and into the EEZ. The arguments made to justify his arrest were that his actions were a danger to himself, other protesters and those working on the *Orient Explorer*. Media reported that one of the conversations that arose in the meetings between government officials and oil and gas industry representatives after the Te Whānau-ā-Apanui flotilla focused on concerns about the lack of 'robust' mechanisms for controlling protestors at sea (see Oil Free Wellington/Scoop 2013; *New Zealand Herald* 2013).

The amendment to the Crown Minerals Act was dubbed the Anadarko Amendment after the Texan oil corporation that was active in Aotearoa New Zealand at the time and was also a silent partner to the Deep Water Horizon rig responsible for the massive spill in the Gulf of Mexico (Smellie 2013). The Amendment imposed exclusion zones around any oil and gas exploration or drill ship, with criminal convictions and large fines for individuals (up to NZ$50,000) and groups (up to NZ$100,000) or twelve months imprisonment for those that breached the zone (Green Party/Scoop 2013; Bond, Diprose and Thomas 2019). The Amendment also enables the New Zealand Defence Force to make arrests for offences under the Amendment including breaching the exclusion zone. Typically, the defence force have limited powers of arrest, unless under specific emergency legislation in crisis situations. Therefore, the Anadarko Amendment extends military power.

The way in which the legislation was introduced also ensured there was little opportunity for debate. At the time, a number of amendments were being made to the Crown Minerals Act that were largely non-controversial. The specific clauses that criminalised protest at sea were introduced through a 'supplementary order paper' (a document introduced right at the end of the legislative process), ensuring it avoided the scrutiny of a select committee and public submissions. It also meant that the Amendments were not analysed in relation to the New Zealand Bill of Rights Act 1990 (BORA). Former Prime Minister and constitution lawyer, Sir Geoffrey Palmer argued that the amendment was in breach of the BORA as well as international human rights conventions that protect non-violent protest in the name of democratic freedoms (see Currie 2013). The government at this time did not address questions around civil rights, and the legislation was passed in a way that is characteristic of the hurried law making during this period (see Davison 2013).

A SOCIAL LICENCE TO OPERATE

Another notion that emerged in these negotiations, and that demonstrates the dominance of neoliberalism, is the idea that certain values can be traded against others. In particular, the idea that corporations whose activities may have negative impacts on local populations can 'buy' a social licence to operate by donating money or resources to local organisations, like swimming pools, art galleries, or concerts and events. A social licence to operate has been used in a variety of different ways, and often means different things to different users of the term. The concept emerged in the 1990s as mining industries tried to manage public perceptions following a variety of environmentally and socially damaging incidents, and attempted to push less responsible operators to lift their game for the good of the whole industry (Edwards and Trafford 2016). A social licence to operate involves the generalised approval of local communities that the industry can operate. It is a negotiation that is, or ought to be, 'bottom up', from the community, and go beyond the regulatory and legislative requirements placed on industry. It should also be adaptive and ongoing, and may include perceptions of trust, legitimacy, credibility, with benefits and disbenefits evenly distributed, and involve procedural fairness (see Edwards and Trafford 2016). In this way, a social licence to operate is not 'given' or 'achieved', rather it can change as perceptions of an industry change. The adaptability of a social licence to operate also implies that it will differ according to the local social, economic and cultural context within which it is sought.

In Aotearoa New Zealand, as Ruckstuhl et al. (2014) have argued, a social licence necessarily involves meeting obligations under Te Tiriti o Waitangi and the UNDRIP. The fundamental premise, then, of a social licence to operate is the consent of those affected, which in the case of Indigenous people requires meaningful engagement and full, prior informed consent. In the context of Te Tiriti, a genuine process of engagement and consent that reflects Māori sovereignty would see each iwi and hapū (tribal groups and groups within them) deciding first what kind of development they wanted in their area, and inviting interest from there (interview with Ana). However, as Ruckstuhl et al. (2015) argue, despite Te Tiriti, the widespread acknowledgement of the role of Treaty principles and the UNDRIP:

> The reality, however, is very different, with the industry having an extremely poor record when it comes to the meaningful involvement of Indigenous communities on whose land much of the mining and resource extraction operations occur. (p. 82)

A crucial point here is that a company may claim a social licence to operate, or may engage in local activities such as sponsoring social infrastructure and amenities as a means to claim or justify what they think their social licence to operate is, but this is not an actual negotiation and nor is it bottom up. Social licence may be implied, but not actively sought from a community. In the absence of conflict or protest there is no visible negation of this social licence, but that doesn't mean people necessarily agree.

THE OIL FREE CAMPAIGN

The legislative changes and the claim to a social licence to operate discussed above reflect the wider power relations in which petro-capitalism operates. They also highlight how industry lobby groups and the government of the day mobilised their power to control the protest against petroleum exploration activities at sea. They suggest active push-back against those who protest, by drawing on regulation, the legal system, and social norms within the hegemony of neoliberalism. A key characteristic of the roll out of neoliberalism is the merging of corporate power with that of governments, and the privileging of transnational corporations and economic justifications for policy and decision-making (Brown 2010). Another characteristic involves active attempts to depoliticise and limit the space in which dissent against petro-capitalism is enacted and heard. Through these processes the intrinsic value of environments, any long-term vision for the future, and a more ethical or collective human-centred imagination for future alternatives has been eroded. Nevertheless, this time frame (2010–2012) also resulted in an acceleration of the dissent that began on the East Cape with Te Whānau-ā-Apanui and Greenpeace discussed above. As the Free Association (2010) suggest, when spaces for active dissent and democratic engagement are narrowed or cramped, this often acts as a pressure cooker for innovation and increased political activity that enables new alternatives to be imagined. This is what we suggest happened in Aotearoa New Zealand as the Oil Free campaign gained momentum.

Between 2011 and 2012 a number of Oil Free groups emerged around the country. Some took the name of their city or region, such as Oil Free Wellington and Oil Free Otago. Others took on different names that more explicitly reflected broader aims such as Climate Justice Taranaki. Some were following on from specific climate activism, such as the Wellington group that built on momentum established from the 2009 Camp for Climate Action Aotearoa, whereas others were starting from little or no former engagement in climate change protest. Greenpeace Aotearoa had a significant role in supporting the groups, even though each operated autonomously. Nevertheless, the groups were networked through regular online meetings, shared resources and also engaged in co-ordinated national actions.

The Oil Free groups reflect an increase in environmental activism in Aotearoa on climate change. Climate action has gradually gained momentum since the mid-2000s. Different groups have operated on different platforms, adopting a range of tactics, and many have been influenced by or networked with other global ENGOs (environmental non-government organisations) or movements. For example, from the mid-2000s, some climate-focused groups were influenced by the Transition Town movement in the UK and adopted similar models and principles. In 2012, there were over 60 transition towns across the country (http://transitiontowns.nz/archive/groups.htm), though many were short-lived. These groups adopted localisation strategies to decarbonise their communities. Other groups were more explicit in their opposition to fossil fuel dependence. In 2004 the Save Happy Valley Coalition campaign began occupying a site in a remote part of the west coast of the South Island where a new open-cast coal mine was proposed by Solid Energy (a state-owned mining company). Their grounds for opposition were related to conservation and climate change. The initial occupation was short-lived, but a later camp was established near the mine site in 2006, and remained there for three years. The campaign also included a range of other tactics including hanging banners on the Solid Energy head office, protest marches, hunger strikes in trees near the site, blockading coal trains, and locking on to earth-moving equipment (O'Brien 2016). While the campaign did not succeed in stopping the mine from going ahead, it did arguably generate momentum and connectivity across different activist groups opposing fossil fuel extraction.

In 2007 an umbrella group, Coal Action Network Aotearoa (CANA) was established as a national organisation with the primary objective to phase out coal by 2027 and to advocate and act for a just transition (https://coalaction.org.nz/about). Two specific proposals in 2010 resulted in CANA gaining significant momentum and a greater profile among the environmental movement. One involved proposed lignite mines in Southland, and the other was the 2Precious2Mine campaign mentioned in Chapter 2. Further examples that demonstrate the relatively slow, but accelerating rise of climate action in Aotearoa in this period were the Camp for Climate Action in 2009, and the emergence of a youth-led group called Generation Zero. The latter group explicitly opted to work within the political system by directly lobbying politicians at local and central government levels to develop policy and regulate to enable a low carbon future (see Moon 2013). At the time of writing, they have been active for over ten years, and instrumental in lobbying the government to develop a 'Zero Carbon' Act which was brought into law in 2019 (Climate Change Response (Zero Carbon) Amendment Act 2019). Clearly the Oil Free campaign emerged at a time when momentum on climate action within Aotearoa's environmental movement was gaining.

Nevertheless, the kind of delegitimising actions discussed above were not new to those involved in such campaigns. For example, three members of the Save Happy Valley Coalition campaign were sued for defamation by Solid Energy in 2006 after they produced a report that documented a list of instances when Solid Energy had caused environmental degradation. The charges were dropped however, suggesting that there was nothing defamatory in the report. To this, a representative of the campaign stated in a press release that the whole fiasco:

> Shows how mistaken and outrageous those attempts to injunct publication of the report were. The whole case has highlighted how anxious this state owned coal miner is to avoid public criticism and debate on their activities. (http://aotearoa.indymedia.org.nz/feature/display/71693/index.php.html)

The Oil Free campaign can be seen as emerging within a context of growing action on climate change both in Aotearoa New Zealand and from abroad. The tactics engaged in by each regional Oil Free group varied, depending on the composition of the group, the local issues they were combatting, and their specific goals. However, these groups were networked, supported one another, and were supported by larger ENGOs, like Greenpeace Aotearoa and 350 Aotearoa, the national branch of 350.org.

CONCLUSION

The Oil Free campaign emerged within the broader context described in this chapter and in Chapter 2 – of ongoing neoliberalisation, advances and push back against honouring Te Tiriti, and a gradually building movement of climate activists. Social action and activism on climate change during this period deployed a range of strategies and tactics, from working within the existing political system, to radical non-violent direct action. The tactics of delegitimisation that met this growing politicisation were broad ranging. In this chapter we have described the criminalisation of protest against oil and gas exploration at sea. The oil and gas industry lobbied the government to ensure their interests were protected through explicit efforts to close down the spaces of dissent available to activists and crucial to a vibrant democracy. This form of silencing also has a history of being very effective at silencing Indigenous voices struggling for their rights and protection of their lands, waters and taonga (treasured things) as promised in Te Tiriti o Waitangi. In the course of our research several activists noted that rather than silencing them, such actions had the opposite effect, with one suggesting the Anadarko Amendment was like 'a red rag to a bull' (interview with Ross). An external review confirmed the politicising effect of the Amendment, noting that it had motivated some 'organised protest entities, increasing the likelihood of on-the-water protest' (Murdoch 2019). From about 2012, opposition to oil and gas exploration at sea was gaining momentum. But as the next chapter discusses, it is not just politicians and the industry that actively delegitimised action on climate change, the media had a significant role to play too.

4

Taming the Narrative

Mainstream media, such as newspapers, television news and radio played a significant role in public life and environmental politics throughout the twentieth century. While many journalists and news organisations may claim to be 'neutral' or 'independent', reporting on 'reality', and adhering to professional standards, these claims are complex. As many of us instinctively know, media organisations are also in business to 'sell' a product – their story. Therefore they make a whole bunch of decisions around what issues to report on, how to frame these issues, who to give space and voice too, and ultimately, what to print, film or record. Journalists and media organisations also need to maintain an audience to survive, so tend to operate within the bounds of what is considered sayable or legitimate in their society. With the rise of social media over the last ten or so years we have witnessed a shift in the historically one-way transfer of information and reporting that twentieth-century media featured. Now people with social media accounts comment, report, film and respond (often in real time) to events and issues in their societies.

Consequently, the communication and media space has become much more complex, fractured and siloed. Some would argue this creates space for enhanced democracy and engagement. However, others might describe it as opening up spaces for misinformation, hate-speech and insidious forms of discrimination and injustice. Digital communication technologies clearly display opportunities for both. But the power relations in the ways that large social media companies' algorithms shape people's engagement with particular discourses or sets of ideas are worth keeping in mind (although it is beyond the scope of a full discussion here). While much is written about the decline of traditional mainstream media, Aotearoa New Zealand's mainstream media organisations still have considerable reach and influence.

In this chapter we explore how debates around continued investment in fossil fuel extraction and use have played out through mainstream and social media. We show how different people and groups, as well as their ideas and actions get framed and represented. We connect these examples from Aotearoa New Zealand to events and trends happening elsewhere in the world. The focus on media is useful because it reflects back more dominant stories, and the limits on what is sayable in certain contexts, while also providing openings to push beyond these limits. As Chapman (2015) notes, understanding how climate issues are framed and how different subjects are constructed provides useful understandings that can inform future organising, action and tactics.

In Chapter 2 we described the developmentalist agenda the National-led government introduced from 2008 in relation to mineral exploration, including oil and gas. In this chapter we focus on how debates over continued investment in fossil fuels (particularly deep-sea oil and gas) and protest actions, have played out through mainstream and social media. We draw on data from three sources:

- An analysis of mainstream media reporting that focused specifically on deep sea oil and gas between 2010 and 2014. This analysis was undertaken for the four major print newspapers in Aotearoa New Zealand (*Otago Daily Times, The Press, The Dominion Post, The Herald*) and any other items represented on the Stuff website www.stuff.co.nz, an online media outlet for most major print newspapers in Aotearoa New Zealand.
- An analysis of social media (Facebook) following a particularly controversial direct action around divestment from fossil fuels in 2016.
- Interviews with activists who reflect on their experiences of engaging with mainstream and social media, and their attempts to influence framing and reporting.

We use these data to show how conflicts around fossil fuel use reflect wider debates about economic growth, the use of resources, and what it means to live well with other people and the non-human world.

OIL AND GAS REPORTING IN MAINSTREAM MEDIA

From the media analysis, which included 351 articles, four major themes emerged that all demonstrate an attitude that the natural environment is thought of as a resource that is useful for human society's economic

development. These themes emphasised the economic contribution of
oil and gas, the need for research to determine the extent of oil and gas
reserves, the missed opportunities from not developing the sector, and
calls for 'balance' and 'efficiency' in environmental decision-making.
Table 4.1 provides a summary of these four themes with representative
quotes and examples.

Table 4.1   Key themes from newspaper analysis legitimising oil and gas exploration (adapted from Diprose, Thomas and Bond 2016, p. 163)

Key themes	Examples of quotes from the media
Important for economic development.	'Oil and gas exploration could contribute significantly to our economy'. (Donnell and Cheng 2011)
Understanding the resource potential.	'The immediate focus is on increasing exploration activity and on improving the knowledge of our petroleum basins'. (Parata, quoted in Kay 2011)
The resource is under-utilised and under-developed.	'For too long now we have not made the most of the wealth hidden in our hills, under the ground, and in our oceans. It is a priority of this Government to responsibly develop those resources'. (Parata, quoted in Kay 2011)
Technology, best practice, and risk management will protect the environment.	'The companies active in New Zealand already operate to the highest standards when it comes to safety and environmental protection and the regulatory regime is well on its way to matching that commitment'. (*Dominion Post* 2011)

These themes seek to establish and reinforce a kind of pragmatic
realism underpinned by the dominance of neoliberal ideology (as discussed in Chapters 2 and 3) and entwined with a sort of nationalist
stewardship. The themes in Table 4.1, first, reinforce the idea that nature
is an economic resource. Second, they emphasise the 'common sense' of
the argument for deep sea oil and gas exploration and extraction as a
means to gain economic growth through which Aotearoa New Zealand
can secure energy independence – that is the development agenda discussed in the previous chapter. And third, the themes reflect a confidence
and assurance that good practice, adhering to environmental standards,
careful risk assessments, and health and safety procedures are capable of

mitigating any and all risks to the environment or to human wellbeing. The combination of these narratives makes them difficult to contest or question. As alternative framings and protest action emerged, the proponents (including elected politicians) of deep sea oil and gas exploration intensified their efforts to reinforce these narratives and to discredit and limit opponents' voices in different ways – both through legislation changes and mainstream/social media.

Government policy focused on extractives as a plank for economic development (discussed in Chapter 2), legislative changes such as the Anadarko Amendment criminalising protest at sea, and the limited opportunities for public engagement in decisions on extraction at sea

Table 4.2 Key themes from newspaper analysis responding to criticism and protest against oil and gas extraction (adapted from Diprose, Thomas and Bond 2016, p. 165)

Key themes	Examples of quotes from the media
Activists are uninformed about the risks.	'Leaders from New Zealand's $2.8 billion oil and gas sector say the country needs better education about the value of the sector as a "vocal minority" continue to oppose the industry.' (McNicol 2013)
Activists are interfering with legal activities.	'It was disappointing protesters had disrupted the research and Ms Parata [conservative MP] urged them to take a calm and reasoned approach towards the company's rights. "Democracy protects the right to protest but not to the extent of interfering with others' rights," she said.' (*Otago Daily Times* 2011)
Activists at sea are a danger to themselves and others.	'There's always a risk of something going wrong if somebody walks into a safety zone—it's like having an unauthorised person walking into a construction site.' (Theunissen 2013)
Activists and opponents to extraction are hypocrites, greenies and hippies.	'The ignorance of these oil protestors never ceases to amaze me. Yet another photo of these people holding plastic banners, wearing life jackets and inflatable rings all made out of the substance they're protesting against.' (Godfrey 2014)
Opponents to oil and gas are just a vocal minority while the 'silent majority' support government decisions on this issue.	'Key denied there was a large number of people in New Zealand worried about the safety of deep sea oil drilling.' (*Stuff* 2013) 'Most New Zealanders back the Government's plan to increase exploration for oil, gas and minerals, a Herald DigiPoll survey suggests.' (Bennett 2012)

provided for in the EEZ Act (discussed in Chapter 3), met with varied public reaction, mobilisation and opposition. Activists, non-governmental organisations, academics, climate action groups and the general public began to question and critique the government and industry-initiated oil and gas expansion. We saw five themes emerge in mainstream reporting responding to and criticising the protest activity (see Table 4.2).

Through the media reporting, politicians, industry and others sought to frame critics and protesters as uninformed, as overstepping their legal democratic rights, as being a danger to themselves and others, as hypocrites, and as an over-vocal minority who did not represent 'ordinary New Zealanders'. These framings sought to represent critics and protesters as being on the fringes of mainstream society, as deluded, naive and dangerous. Such framings reflect an underlying paternalism that is often used to discredit groups who challenge authority, and reflects historic framings of women, people of colour, LGBTQI people, and those with mental illness, whereby critics and protesters are seen as child-like or feeble-minded who need protecting from their own ill-considered actions (Perone 2014; Kay and Mendes 2020; Brickell 2000). While these framings were partly in response to critics and protestors' actions and arguments, they also sought to limit the debate around oil and gas to managerial issues – risk assessments, managing potential spills and limiting pollution. What was noticeably absent was any mention of how expanded oil and gas use would increase anthropogenic climate change.

CONTESTING GOVERNMENT AND OIL INDUSTRY NARRATIVES

Activists were well aware of these framings and limits. A common theme that emerged through interviews (at that time, in the mid-2010s) was the difficulty of campaigning on climate change. For as one activist said:

> [C]limate change needs a paradigm shift. I mean, there is no other way to get out of it without entirely changing the way that we do business globally, and that's huge. That's why it's exciting. It's also why it's daunting and it's also why the anti-climate change movement, for want of a better term, is all over the place. (Interview with Ross)

As a result of the enormity of climate change, in the mid-2010s Oil Free groups used a range of tactics in their dissent and tended to avoid referring to climate change itself. Nevertheless, they still sought to challenge both the industry and the government in the way that they framed these forms of pragmatic realism, nationalism and managerialism. Activists sought to frame extraction at sea as irresponsible and in doing so asserted a sense of care and hope for a low carbon future. Yet they were mindful of securing support in their campaign, which at the time of interviewing, focused on two strategies. In the first, activists highlighted the intrinsic value of non-human environments that New Zealanders are typically passionate about, and emphasised the threat that deep sea oil drilling poses to them. Thus they sought to mobilise New Zealanders' care for the kinds of places they love, and drew on a kind of eco-nationalism. The second strategy drew in high-profile but 'average New Zealanders' to make their eco-nationalist arguments against deep sea oil more accessible to a wider audience, transcending both the dominance of economic arguments about jobs and growth as well as any political allegiance to left or right. We focus on these two strategies in the next two subsections.

Mobilising Care Through Eco-identity Narratives

One way activists sought to mobilise people to join them in opposing deep sea oil was by emphasising the risks of oil spills to beaches and coastal environments, drawing on the 'no drill, no spill' slogan. Activists organised protest flotillas at sea, some of which deliberately breached ocean exclusion zone rules legislated through the so-called Anadarko Amendment that followed Te Whānau-ā-Apanui's actions (see Chapter 3). They also organised 'Oil Free Summits', held local events like 'Banners on the Beach', issued press releases, tried to disrupt oil industry meetings, and protested at city ports and outside oil companies' offices (see for instance, O'Neil 2014; *3 News* 2014). Despite the diversity of these actions, and the local nature of many of them, they all drew on the idea that all New Zealanders are passionate about and value pristine beaches. One activist described it as:

> Values based campaigning, and the values have been deemed that New Zealanders want to go to the beach, they want to ... have a picnic, they want to catch a fish for dinner, and these are values that all New Zealanders hold dear. It cuts across the left/right spectrum. It doesn't matter who you are, we all want to go to the beach. (Interview with Ross)

Another activist described this as reflecting an entrenched cultural identity, 'a story that we tell ourselves' (Interview with Vicki). Activists suggested that connections with beaches were a key part of 'who we are' as New Zealanders, and this became a key narrative of opposition to deep sea drilling and a strong mobilising factor. The 2011 *Rena* disaster in Tauranga (discussed in Chapter 3) was often mentioned by activists as an emotive and highly visible example that really drove home the risks posed by deep sea oil, through images of seabirds smeared in black goop and polluted spoiled beaches. It also raised questions about the capacity of the government (and industry) in resourcing a clean-up in the event of a larger spill further offshore. For example, one interviewee suggested:

> [The] threat of oil spills is a pretty big deal for people. I think especially after seeing the *Rena* spill over in Tauranga, people have a much more tangible sense of what that actually means. I went over there with a bunch of volunteers and was involved in the clean-up. We talked to the communities there and heard a lot about the impact that they suffered, and just for the whole country it's much more tangible now than it ever was before. (Interview with Vicki)

The narrative created drew on an idea that all New Zealanders are universally passionate and care about beaches. This kind of eco-nationalist narrative that appeals to, and reinforces 'universal values' can be exclusionary, and may reflect dominant values, such as those inherent to colonialism or those in privileged positions who can access regular beach holidays. They also create an image of pristine nature that is people-less, underpinned by the Western view of nature as separate from humans (see, for instance, Willems-Braun 1997; Ginn 2008; Finney 2014; Bond, Diprose and McGregor 2015). We discuss the problematic characteristics of this Western-centric separation between nature and humans and how it is exacerbated through the dominance of neoliberalism further in Chapter 7. While some activists were acutely aware of these aspects of the kind of eco-nationalist narratives they drew on, they still found it to be a useful strategy, perhaps because of their very dominance. By appealing to the passion the majority of New Zealanders are assumed to have, activists drew out an emotional connection to non-human nature that itself worked to contradict the pragmatic realism of economic growth through resource extraction and managerialism that underpins the development agenda of the government and industry. Focusing on the importance of beaches and coastal environments to national identity also hinted at the intrinsic value of these environments, and the entanglement of the environment, people's wellbeing, lifestyle and identity even within the Western framing that separates people and nature. The campaign sought to mainstream the idea that these places should not be risked even if it promotes economic development or employment. The activists sought to pose moral and ethical questions, as suggested by one activist:

> The conversation needs to move to 'what sort of a society are we?' Are we a society that just pursues the almighty dollar regardless of the consequences? Are we prepared to sell our beaches and our way of life, but moreover, the entire planet for the pursuit of short term gains? And that conversation needs to be happening. And it is, but not to a large extent. And when we've got people saying, 'Yeah, actually no, this is just wrong,' then the legislation doesn't matter. (Interview with Ross)

Mobilising 'Average New Zealanders'

The second strategy, mobilising 'average New Zealanders' in local communities was another key approach Oil Free groups used. This approach sought to generate local community opposition to reduce oil companies' social licence to operate (see Chapters 3 and 5 for further discussion). Interview participants noted that the campaign was about generating 'social and cultural resistance within your community so when these oil companies choose to set up here commercially, they're not welcome' (interview with Kiri). Several participants also noted that the media tended to present a discourse that was disparaging of environmentalists, suggesting they were crazy, lefty hippies (see Phelan and Shearer 2009). This awareness led to an alternative strategy within the campaign, whereby they actively sought out 'respectable' community leaders who would represent 'average' New Zealanders and who could take prominent roles in actions. These were considered useful ways to draw in more support for climate action by those who might not normally engage in activism or social action.

This kind of strategy is often adopted in social movements as one that seeks to 'credentialise' participants (Benford and Snow 2000; O'Brien 2015). For example, as noted by one activist, engaging and profiling 'respectable' community members in a flotilla that gained a high profile enabled people to:

> see that you don't have to be a crazy leftie or have a pile of dreadlocks or anything to oppose deep sea oil drilling. You've got reverends, pro-

fessors and ministers and old women … And if you're an everydayer
that wants to say no, that's fine because these big names … they are also
doing it … Because I think that the [emergence of a group supporting
gas exploration and extraction] have marginalised a lot of the people
in the middle of the ground. You know, they've made it, if you say no to
deep sea drilling, they think you're also saying no to economic growth
and to jobs … So being able to bring out these enormous huge names
in saying no, is a way – our way to counter that. (Interview with Kiri)

In addition to the strategy of 'credentialising' the campaign, the activists
we interviewed were also aware of the benefits of localised, but nationally
supported, actions. For example, in 2013, an action called Banners on the
Beach was co-ordinated nationally, in that resources and support were
provided, but local groups around the country could initiate and organise
actions locally. Although efforts to delegitimise the action occurred
through sound bites like the then Prime Minister John Key describing
the numbers as 'modest', and the participants in the action as a 'Greenpeace rent-a-crowd' (cited in Satherley 2013), the broader benefits of the
campaign were less outwardly tangible, but still significant. The local
actions by about 40–50 organisers around the country generated solidarity and support that provided the motivation and momentum for the
campaign to endure. One interviewee recalled that for one local organ-
iser, who was relatively new to such work, the 500-strong turnout gave
'them a huge amount of courage just knowing that all these people were
on side and do support and do believe in the same things' (Interview with
Vicki).

Through highlighting the importance of specific places to people's
sense of identity, and building local opposition to deep sea oil drilling and
exploration in those specific local places, activists created what Benford
and Snow (2000) call 'narrative fidelity'. This refers to the way these activists sought to engage 'average New Zealanders' at the local level in the
very places they valued – local beaches to legitimise and give strength
to their narratives. Through this narrative fidelity activists sought to
counter the pragmatic realist (nature as resource for economic growth)
framing of the government and oil industry by mobilising people to see
this as a risk to the places they love and value, and by extension their
sense of identity and meaning. It is clear that there existed a constant
effort on one side to delegitimise and discredit the campaign, followed
by a push-back and adaptation by the activists to find alternate ways to

repoliticise and legitimise opposition against deep sea oil extraction. Our interview participants were well aware of this constant tension and the need to keep pushing and finding alternate ways to maintain their visibility and momentum despite the risks both emotionally and sometimes (as discussed below and in Chapter 6) physically. As one activist noted:

> You only need a few people in the community to go 'drilling sucks, drilling sucks, drilling sucks' that it creates a tone where people go, 'actually yeah, drilling sucks', and change their mind and hopefully shut it down. But it can work the other way too you know. You don't ever own it. (Interview with Kiri)

LIMITATIONS OF THE CAMPAIGN FRAMING

Even at the time of interviewing, activists were keenly aware of the limitations of their strategies, particularly the eco-nationalist messaging around 'no drill, no spill' and the threat to beaches. Some were ambivalent, seeing the strategy as useful in mobilising the public around what was seen as a common concern. However, they recognised that it limited their ability to raise climate change more directly as the primary issue. Others have highlighted the difficulty in bringing local concerns and a sense of responsibility to what, in the mid-2010s, was seen as an intangible global (and therefore remote and irrelevant) phenomena (Usher 2013; O'Brien 2015, 2016). We pick up on this thread in Chapter 7, but in the context of the tactics used in the Oil Free campaign at this time, some activists we spoke to felt the focus on beaches and coastlines was misdirected, reactionary, and failed to initiate discussion on the important issues associated with climate justice. One example that highlighted this discontent occurred in Ōtepoti Dunedin, where modelling showed that an oil spill would be unlikely to affect local east coast beaches, but would rather drift towards Rekohu/Wharekauri, the Chatham Islands which lie 800 km off the east coast of the South Island. An activist indicated that many:

> people were like 'oh, ok, sweet' and I was like 'Ah NO, no, no!' that's not what we're trying to say… I mean, really economics and climate are the big ones, and as a group [we] have to push that a lot more. (Interview with Olivia)

While the activists' sought to open up debate on issues of climate change, such messaging did little to shift debate toward matters that they considered the most important. One activist suggested 'you can't own the renewables and that's the problem. So that's why there is no transition. You can't make as much money out of renewables as you can make out of fossil fuels' (interview with Ricky). While all campaigns have limitations because of the need to balance messaging with the need to engender public support, these issues also speak to the specific complexity connected to climate action, at a time in the mid-2010s, when many middle-class New Zealanders were still not keen to be confronted by climate realities.

Notwithstanding these limitations, the Oil Free campaign did mobilise people across Aotearoa New Zealand through the eco-nationalist identity narratives that were used. Activists emphasised the inherent value of non-human things (beaches) as interconnected with a sense of national identity, suggesting that all New Zealanders want to protect beaches and coastlines and to contest any threats posed them, despite the pragmatic realism and managerialist assurances of the government and oil industry. The eco-nationalist identity, along with the support of 'average New Zealanders' fronting campaign actions provided an entry point for members of the public to get involved, be concerned and express this concern publicly. Deep sea drilling was not just about the threat to beaches it was about 'who we are', a threat to New Zealand identity itself. These strategies highlighted the connection between place and action and the entanglement between the human and non-human worlds. The place-identity narratives that activists articulated, while rooted in the local, also transcend this scale, and provided one path to care and act about climate change in Aotearoa New Zealand.

LOSING THE NARRATIVE

Not all actions that the Oil Free groups in our study engaged in were effective in holding onto the narrative opposing oil and gas extraction. One example occurred in Ōtepoti Dunedin, a small city on the southeast coast of the South Island where activists were involved in blockading banks as part of 350.org's 'Breakfree from Fossil Fuel' global divestment campaign in 2016. Again, we have reported on this elsewhere, focusing on the tension between the violence meted out to activists and the violence of inaction on climate change more generally (see Diprose et al. 2017). Here, we use the same data to highlight the way in which mainstream print media, social media and policing combined to push back against activist work that dissents against business-as-usual.

The Aotearoa New Zealand engagement in the divestment campaign involved a series of blockades at ANZ banks around the country on different days. The ANZ Bank is among the largest of the main banks that operate in the country, and was chosen as a target because it was claimed they had NZ$13 billion of investments in fossil fuels.[1] While these actions were peaceful, largely resulting in banks remaining closed for the day and disrupting business-as-usual, the Ōtepoti Dunedin action became a flashpoint illustrating how climate activists not only lost control of their narrative, but also became subject to abuse and violence. In what follows we show how the framing of activists in this example reinforces the point made above about how activists are delegitimised in the media and how such dehumanising ways of thinking of activists and those who dissent are used to justify violence against them.

The action itself involved a group of approximately 130–180 climate activists blockading the front entrances of three ANZ banks in downtown Ōtepoti Dunedin. The action began with activists meeting in the centre of the city before opening hours and walking towards two ANZ branches on opposite corners of George Street (the main street) and Hanover Street. Activists described how the action began peacefully with groups at the two branches on opposite sides of the road, and pedestrians and motorists showing their support. The banks remained closed. The activists then decided to blockade a third ANZ branch in the central city two blocks away, so small groups from the two existing blockades splintered off to go to the third bank that was now open for business for the day. Once the third bank was blockaded, it remained open, and the other two banks then also opened. This marked a significant difference from similar actions held earlier in the month in other centres around Aotearoa New Zealand in that those banks remained closed for the duration of protest action. Following this decision to blockade the third bank and the banks opening for business, things shifted.

Two things occurred simultaneously. First, it seemed that some agreement was made between the ANZ Bank and the police, in that protesters were not arrested and removed. Instead, police encouraged members of the public to use 'reasonable force' to cross the barricade. This was interpreted literally by some members of the public who were violent in their efforts to access the bank. While some activists were unsurprised at police violence directed at them, they did not expect the police to encourage members of the public to be violent toward them (discussed further in Chapter 6). Second, the media portrayal replicated and reproduced the way in which activists in this action were delegitimised. Only eight articles were published nationally in the mainstream media on the 'Break Free' campaign. Five of those were specifically on the Ōtepoti Dunedin actions and these were written with a significant difference in tone. The three articles on the wider campaign, published prior to events in Ōtepoti Dunedin paid significant attention to 350.org's arguments and did so fairly sympathetically. However, as several activists noted, there was a major shift when it came to reporting on the actions in Ōtepoti Dunedin. This shift occurred when an older woman was filmed by the media being helped across the blockade to one of the banks. Despite the existence of an easily accessible side door, and encouragement by several ANZ employees and activists to use it, the police (according to activists interviewed) insisted on supporting her while she climbed over the seated activists in the blockade. The video footage and images of this were immediately posted to Facebook and then shortly after to the local mainstream online newspaper site, *The Otago Daily Times*. From this moment, the content began to describe the 'disrespectful' activists, who 'forced' the elderly woman to clamber over them to do her weekly banking. The comments on the Facebook post were vitriolic, labelling activists as 'a bunch of retards', 'society's losers' and a 'bunch of dickheads'. In contrast, police were 'balanced', 'compelled' to help the woman, as an ordinary citizen, to undertake their everyday activities (Elder 2016). ANZ branches were similarly presented in a positive light – respectful of the right to free speech and to protest but concerned for the safety of staff and customers, and were presented as taking seriously issues of climate change through various actions of their own (Lin 2016; Stewart 2016).

The activists' recollections and experiences of these events were quite different. For example, of the elderly woman, they reported:

she came out to us and was saying horrible stuff to us, and like flicking us with her cane … And then the cop was encouraging her to go through, and like she could barely walk, why would you encourage her to go through when there's a side door? And I felt like it was just a set-up. And then later on, another old lady came up and then the camera was like positioned all ready for it, and it just felt set up. (Interview with George)

Similarly, a blog posted by activist Siana Fitzjohn who was involved in the actions in Ōtepoti Dunedin, summed up the effect of the way the media framed these events:

> The coverage successfully removed responsibility [for environmental harm] from ANZ and the police, who worked together to create that scenario. … as a group we need to take responsibility for the collateral damage of our actions. When we're going against powerful institutions we will inconvenience people, people will take it personally, and we will hurt people's feelings. That is the unfortunate reality of direct action, and it does upset us. But the damage being done by the prevailing status quo is far more immense, far more devastating and far more invisible. (Fitzjohn 2016)

The media framed activists as disrespectful, unemployable, young and irresponsible as a result of the disruption to 'innocent' citizens. It situated the activists in opposition to bank customers. This was counter to the intentions of 350.org campaign that sought to 'scale up' debate by opposing and highlighting the complicit nature of banks as prominent and powerful capitalist institutions that are complicit in propping up, profiting from, and supporting petro-capitalism. Clearly in this instance, activists lost control of their messaging. The result was that the action actually 'scaled down' debate through this shift in focus from banks to customers and ordinary citizens and away from the complicity that individuals and collective society have in enabling the network of institutions that support climate changing sectors like the petroleum industry to continue to operate. It also avoided conversation or debate about the individual and collective vulnerability of society to climate change impacts (Randall 2005). For example, one activist recalled:

> People couldn't quite register the fact that you know there's a vast difference between us making the day of a couple of people a bit more inconvenient, versus climate change killing people, and like making people lose their homes, like that's considerably more inconvenient than not being able to get into a bank for the day when there's another one just down the road. (Interview with Frankie)

In Chapter 2, we noted that one of the core tenets of neoliberalism is the realignment of the definition of freedom to refer to individual market freedom and economic choice. The framing of the activists and the violence by the police and local bank users toward activists demonstrates this shift. Consumer choice and individual freedom is privileged as the only 'legitimate' response to climate change action. After this action in Ōtepoti Dunedin, activists reflected on some of the decisions they had made. In hindsight, they recognised that they were more likely to have retained control of their key message had they not moved to blockade the third bank. That the bank was already open shifted the dynamic, and is likely to have been the catalyst that prompted the first two banks, that had initially stayed closed, to open. Several activists commented that they felt this was the moment when the media presentations began to reconstruct the conflict from one between the activists and the bank, in the context of complicit support for the fossil fuel industry, to a conflict between the activists and members of the public (interviews with Dan, Rieley, Kate, Rachel and John). The activists also thought about how they might have responded or adapted when police began to encourage people to use 'reasonable force' against them. For example, they could have stood up or gone into the bank and adopted different tactics that focused the attention on the bank and activists rather than activists and public/police (interviews with Dan, Kate and Riley).

CONCLUSION

This chapter has shown how the media (and policing) forms part of the broader set of processes across society that produce and reproduce the push-pull in a campaign. On one hand, issues campaigned on are polit-icised through actions, positive media responses (that engage with and debate the issues), awareness raising and education. On the other hand, and simultaneously, issues and activists are managed and depoliticised through a range of tactics. For example, legislative changes can restrict formal mechanisms for engagement, pushing people into non-violent direct actions and criminalisation can shape activists' willingness to engage in actions. Activists' actions can also be delegitimised and disci-plined through media portrayals and societal responses and sometimes activists' bodies are even dehumanised through violence (as some of our participants referred to feeling in the ANZ action – also see Chapter 6). These tactics of silencing dissent enable the hegemony of neoliberal business-as-usual to endure. The media, both mainstream and social media, operate in complex ways to shift the terms of debate away from those that contest or dissent against business-as-usual. This enables easy recourse to arguments that privilege jobs and the economy over human and non-human wellbeing. The media also provides a means to legitimise some bodies such as people going to the bank, especially if they are older women wielding canes caught on camera, against so-called unemployed 'dickheads' and hippies. Similarly, the media enables a way of framing what it means to be responsible and who can be responsible, of supporting individuals who represent 'good ordinary citizens' and by implication protecting business-as-usual. The above examples highlight the role of institutions like the police in these depoliticising tactics. The next two chapters continue to identify further ways in which attempts are made to manage and control dissent, resulting in the push-pull in a campaign.

5

Securing Business-as-usual

SECURITISATION

During the time period of our research, the oil and gas industry and the national government in Aotearoa New Zealand had worked to increase the certainty of doing fossil fuel business here. As we've written about in Chapters 2 and 3, this involved things like legislative changes that criminalise protest and reduce consultation obligations. It also involved practices of securitisation. Dalby (2002, p. 163) defines security as being:

> about the future or fears about the future. It is about contemporary dangers but also thwarting potential future dangers. It is about control, certainty, predictability in an uncertain world, and, in attempting to forestall chance and change it is frequently a violent practice.

Through the legislative changes, for example, the government attempted to make more certain the investment conditions for oil and gas companies and industry. In addition, the Petroleum Exploration and Production Association of New Zealand (PEPANZ), the industry lobby group, sought to influence the government to make secure their business environment. However, the security enjoyed by the industry was threatened by the growing number of communities and groups who were organising against expanded oil and gas exploration and extraction, and arguing for climate justice. Through campaigning and direct action, these communities and groups represented a persistent danger to the oil and gas industry and particularly for the New Zealand government, as they undermined the attractiveness of the country for international investors.

Uncertain climate futures and politics are also threats to security. Climate justice movements have argued that climate futures bring into sharp relief social injustice, given that those most affected by climate change are least responsible for generating emissions. We can understand climate politics and calls for justice then, as an area that reveals different, often competing, practices that seek the security of something or some group. The key question in a feminist geopolitical framing is 'security for whom?' So in this chapter, we are interested in the ways different actors sought to control against fears and create certainty. This includes the oil and gas industry, along with the state who have played a role in trying to control the politics of this issue. But it also includes activists who engaged in their own practices of trying to be secure and mitigate fears, at the same time as destabilising the dependence on fossil fuels and business-as-usual so that different environmental and economic formations might flourish. Feminist geopolitics, the approach we described in Chapter 1, is a useful way of understanding competing practices that seek security from uncertain futures because it embraces the diversity of actors and processes. This chapter explores two particular strategies of securitisation – corporate social responsibility (CSR) and practices of surveillance.

CORPORATE SOCIAL RESPONSIBILITY AS SECURITISATION

As the climate rapidly changes, the oil and gas industry grapples with questions about corporate social responsibility (CSR). Much of the literature analysing the emergence of CSR has focused on developing country contexts, and in particular on the oil sector in the Niger Delta (Moen and Lambrechts 2013; Frynas 2005) where transnational corporations in alliance with the Nigerian government have gained a reputation for exploitative activities and environmental degradation (see Watts 2004). The CSR discourses that have been dominant since the mid-2000s begin from the assumption that 'CSR initiatives that contribute to sustainable development have the potential to address local grievances and improve community livelihoods', thereby managing political (and environmental) risk (Moen and Lambrechts 2013, p. 98). Banks et al. (2016, p. 253) argue that corporate involvement in community development can oscillate between genuine accountability, a public relations (PR) strategy and 'conflict avoidance'. In this context, an initiative that is more akin to a PR strategy might be specifically spinning a partial truth in order to place the business in a favourable light. Likewise, a business may avoid presenting all the information in order to avoid conflict and protect the brand and, therefore, shareholders' assets. As external pressure mounts on a business or industry, these tactics may become increasingly aggressive or even violent in order to secure the company's future. In different moments and in different contexts, companies may move between motivations, and they might not be mutually exclusive. These different rationales, and the effects of them, were apparent within the oil and gas exploration and extraction sector in Aotearoa New Zealand.

At the time of our research, there were twelve different companies engaged in offshore exploration and extraction. Only two of these companies responded to our invitations to be interviewed, plus a member of the industry lobby group PEPANZ. These interviews gave valuable insights, but it was also apparent from media reporting and interviews with community members that there were significant variations across all companies in how they understood and engaged 'responsibly'. Some companies were renowned for their poor community engagement, particularly with Māori, while other companies had carefully built networks in the towns and cities onshore from their operational sites. The industry lobby group representative said that although the practices and approaches varied, most companies engage communities well beyond what is required:

Adrian: It's an active part of decision making, 'what's the impact going to be on this community?' Legally, I can just go and do whatever I want because I've met all the regulatory requirements but it's not really the answer.

Amanda: Do you think most companies go beyond that?

Adrian: Definitely.

He went on to give examples of companies sending residents on holiday during periods of noisy onshore work, gifting land to a local rugby union, supporting schools with traffic management. When asked why these companies would go beyond the legal requirements, he stated that 'It's the ethos of the industry ... It recognises that it's a part of that community and therefore it has an obligation to play an active part' (interview with Adrian).

One company that participated in our research purposefully emphasised their place-based connections and roots in Aotearoa New Zealand. This was partly a strategy to make themselves attractive to multinational companies that might need a partner to tap in to the networks of a company already established here. They promoted themselves as the 'New Zealand partner of choice', and 'that's something we should really promote and build off is the fact that we've got local networks, local people' (interview with Kelly). This particular company had hired a community engagement manager and set up community panels in areas where they were working. The community panels were made up of people invited by the company and representing a range of sectors, 'youth, local business, social service providers ... NGO[s], iwi ... conservation people and then like [a] local Lions [service-based community group] rep or something like that' (interview with Kelly). Kelly reported that iwi participation was uneven with some iwi wanting to take part, some wanting to stay informed and some not wanting to be lumped in with other 'stakeholders' and, instead, asking for a more direct relationship with the company. The purpose of these panels was to provide:

a conduit for community feedback to our company and so that we have sort of checks and balances in the community perspective in the same way that shareholders contact our investor relations people and go 'what are you doing about the – why is this, why did you decide to do [that]' ... so that we can hear the community voice. And so purposely we're not trying to create cheerleaders ... Likewise we get their input into things like contribution to community, so sponsorship and partnerships and things like that. (Interview with Kelly)

One of the things that made this approach unique was the long-term commitment this company seemingly made to building relationships. One of the community panels had been set up in an area they were not yet extracting from. 'It's a bit of a luxury in this kind of role to genuinely be doing the long-term stuff' (interview with Kelly). The input of community groups 'in theory makes the business a stronger, more resilient business because you're in touch, you know your risks, you know your opportunities' (interview with Kelly). This can also be seen as an effort to mitigate risk, conflict or protest, and to claim the benefits of local engagement and consultation that endorses their activities. Prno and Slocombe (2012) argue that local communities present a latent threat – if they're unhappy with a company's activities, they can disrupt them through boycott or direct action. Ana, a research participant who worked for an iwi affected by exploration, talked about oil and gas companies' fears of an 'iwi veto'. As we discussed in Chapter 2, this is not something that actually exists in legislation, but demonstrates the (perceived at least) social power of Māori activism. It becomes increasingly important, therefore, to secure communities' consent to avoid 'potentially costly conflict and exposure to social risks' (Prno and Slocombe 2012, p. 346).

Another company set up a corporate responsibility committee where they weighed up proposals for, what they call, social sponsorship. Projects they've funded in the past include whale surveys, wetland restoration and meeting house insulation. These projects were localised to areas where they are exploring or extracting:

> One of the key drivers [of what gets funded] is to make sure that sponsorship is occurring in a place where we'd have effects or we have some sort of potential operational influence. (Interview with Jamie)

The participant from this company characterised their relationships with communities as good, in contrast to other companies:

> You hear it through some of the other operators around, why has [this company] got such a good relationship with some of their stakeholders? And it really does come down to resourcing and good groundwork and being quite open and transparent with what we're doing. (Interview with Jamie)

Jamie said that CSR was 'the right thing to do' rather than being about making business easy.

These efforts outlined above were about securing a social licence to operate (see Chapter 3). Adrian, from the industry lobby group, said:

> we use [social licence] as shorthand for trust ... you don't have to like this activity but we have to earn the trust of the communities in which we operate. We are going to be open and transparent and honest with you. We are going to listen to what you say. We are going to seek to incorporate that ... It's about everybody.

However, it seemed unclear how a company would actually know if they had a licence to operate, or what it would mean for a community to revoke that licence, as shown in the interview with Adrian:

> Amanda: How does a company know that they have got that kind of mandate from the community to be operating? For example, Kaikōura where there has been an active group, No Drill Kaikōura.
>
> Adrian: Because they talk to people and they get told 'don't come to Kaikōura'. Well, if we're not wanted here, we're not going

to be here ... I can't think off the top of my head of other examples but I'm sure there are ... it's going to be really hard to operate if that community don't want you there.

Shortly after however, he stated:

Adrian: There's a group of residents at Tikorangi who are strongly opposed [to onshore drilling]. Well, that doesn't mean all of Tikorangi is opposed.

Amanda: How does that get weighed up?

Adrian: Ultimately that's regulatory ... So there's one avenue there, but more importantly it's about saying well everyone has the opportunity to talk to the company and the company is going to take all those views into account and when it makes its decision [that] we are going to stay here, it's done in the full knowledge that a particular group are opposed to that and they'll seek to mitigate the impacts on them in the same way they'll mitigate it on everybody else ... I mean if it's strongly opposed on ideological or belief grounds, it doesn't really matter how much traffic re-routing you do right?

In this answer, Adrian demonstrates that although CSR and social licence are promoted as going beyond regulatory requirements, these regulatory requirements are, nevertheless, viewed as the final arbiter of a licence to operate and a planning consent is ultimately enough. This is contrary to the understanding of social licence we discussed in Chapter 3, where we suggested that it involves an adaptive, generalised 'bottom up' approval negotiated by local communities reflecting trust, procedural fairness and the even distribution of negative and positive effects of the activity (Edwards and Trafford 2016). It was also noted, that it goes beyond regulatory and legislative requirements.

A similar retreat to regulation came through when we asked industry representatives about how corporate social responsibility relates to climate change:

Amanda: When it comes to stuff around climate change and corporate social responsibility, how do you engage with that?

Kelly: So [this] company did some market research ... but interestingly, climate change didn't come up as an issue at all. It was not on the radar ... It's obviously hot for core groups but across that middle New Zealand, it's not.

A related answer was given when another exploration company representative was asked the same question:

Amanda: Within the context of climate change, does that change how you engage with corporate social responsibility?

Jamie: Not really in New Zealand at the moment ... you're led by whatever the government's going to be doing and your input into those processes but it's not the big driver in New Zealand.

At first glance, this makes sense. It would be quite contradictory for the fossil fuel industry to take leadership on climate change beyond government policy or what most New Zealanders want within the context of petro-capitalism. But the approach to the Tikorangi community and response to climate change are at odds with Adrian's characterisation of CSR going beyond regulatory requirements and a concern for the impacts on each community. In both quotes above, the sector falls back on regulation as the default, and 'community' is carefully defined in a way that limits who the companies are responsible to in executing their CSR. CSR is not for those who are 'strongly opposed on ideological or belief grounds'. It is, as Adrian goes on to say, for 'middle New Zealand' which is:

the sort of shorthand for the group in the middle, the general public. You know, because actually in a parliamentary democracy, that's who decides. The voting middle decide. Yes, they're influenced by those at the end but if you want a change of government, it's that group in the middle that decide. It's not the 'stick in the muds' at either end of the spectrum. So you know, they're clearly a focus for everybody to communicate [with]. (Interview with Adrian)

CSR was further limited by the way that some of the industry participants argued that their product itself was a demonstration of CSR. At the root of the fossil fuel industry's arguments that they were being responsible to communities was the idea that:

we're producing a product that people demand still. Not just for transport and energy but I'm sure parts of your clothes, parts of my clothes, lots of things in your home have a component based on hydrocarbon[s]. (Interview with Adrian)

Adrian talked about 'energy equity', providing the security of supply so that 'we can live the lives we want to live'. This construction of CSR was apparent when the industry was particularly threatened, for instance when there were direct actions or the prospect of different regulatory settings. For instance, when legislative changes in 2018 heralded the beginning of the end for offshore exploration, the industry group's response was to promote gas as central to energy security, a kiwi way of life (like barbeques) and necessary to any 'just transition'. The energy from oil and gas is 'fundamental to our way of life', the CEO of the oil and gas lobby group argued (*Stuff* 2018), and the centre-right National party's spokesperson for energy and resources worried that in '10 years' time we will be buying imported gas to fire up the barbecue' (Watson 2018). The way hydrocarbons are embedded into daily life was repeatedly used to dismiss and undermine activists. Kelly was wary of the depoliticising effects of this though:

We're providing an energy service but it's big stuff and the risks are big and I think a bit of protest is very, very healthy and important. And I *hate* industry pulling the easy card and saying, you know, 'protestors should be cycling and working by candlelight and drove here in their petrol driven vehicles and blah blah blah'.

CSR was understood in a range of sometimes contradictory ways by industry representatives, from invoking a social licence to operate by suggesting efforts to go beyond legislative requirements for working with communities, through to simply arguing that the provision of fossil fuels for daily life is their responsibility. Media often cited companies stating that protestors had a right to their views, and to legal protest. However, when extractive industry CSR is criticised, the industry often responds with surveillance as a method of securitisation.

TRACING SURVEILLANCE

As noted at the beginning of this chapter, the certainty and security the oil and gas industry were used to operating in shifted with the rise of climate justice activism globally. Another approach to making the industry more secure, and increasing the certainty that investors and companies seek, is through surveillance. This serves to 'anticipate and contain' actions that might render their activities uncertain (Hansen and Uldam 2015, p. 187). David Lyon (2001, p. 6) writes that '[s]urveillance is the means whereby knowledge is produced for administering populations in relation to risk', or in other words, a risk management strategy which involves collecting information about people who pose a risk. Jennifer Robinson (2000) points to the diverse ways that surveillance power plays out. While acknowledging the dominant trope of an all-seeing panopticon, she also describes surveillance as being bound up with relationships of care, for instance, neighbours keeping an eye on each other. However, Lyon describes a creeping normalisation of surveillance and the way knowledge gathering has been justified for the purpose of managing risks related to 'obtaining compliance or containing threatening behaviour' (Lyon 2001, p. 6). The power embedded in surveillance activities, especially in efforts to control and manage unwanted behaviour, are experienced unevenly by different groups. For instance, communities of colour and Indigenous communities are often portrayed as particularly 'risky' or 'threatening' and so are subjected to increased surveillance.

Like traditional geopolitics, much surveillance literature has focussed on the state. But Eveline Lubbers (2015) has called for more nuanced studies that explore the increasingly blurry relationship between the state and private companies in practices of surveilling activists. She details the long history of state/corporate relationships that have quashed resistance to capitalist practices (see also Dalby 2015), including the revelations in the UK of police infiltration of activist groups, for instance, London Greenpeace in the 1980s as they organised against McDonalds. Valerie Morse (2019a) similarly traces the way surveillance has targeted those who resist the expansion of neoliberal relations in Aotearoa New Zealand.

In our case study, there were complex intersecting relationships between private companies within the extractive industries, the state, and private security companies. These interweavings are not new in Aotearoa New Zealand but they are often opaque and unseen by the general population. An anti-coal mining group, Save Happy Valley, was infiltrated in the 2000s by private security company Thompson and Clark who were working for a state-owned enterprise (*Sunday Star Times* 2009). The same practice was used in a campaign led by a PR firm in the late 1990s against a group opposing native timber-logging. Hager and Burton (1999, p. 2) wrote that the PR firm, Shandwick, and its clients, 'infiltrated environment groups and systematically attacked critics and potential critics of the logging industry including journalists, academics and even grade school principals'. In 2017 Greenpeace New Zealand revealed it had been leaked information showing that their activists and workers had been under almost daily surveillance for years. This involved being followed and photographed in their regular lives (Taylor 2017).

As Greenpeace investigated, they sought to unpick the different relationships involved in this surveillance. Thompson and Clark again were the security agency leading the surveillance. The company describes themselves as 'New Zealand's leading security, corporate intelligence and protection agency' (Thompson and Clark n.d.), and have been hired in recent years by the petroleum industry lobby group and oil and gas companies, like OMV, whose largest shareholder is the Austrian government (Hager 2021). Greenpeace New Zealand sought information about what was going on through an Official Information Act (OIA) request, which is a legal mechanism by which anyone can request information that involves government or public agencies' activities (when certain criteria are met). The Greenpeace New Zealand Director, and former Green Party Member of Parliament, Russel Norman said:

> We asked for copies of emails from Thompson and Clark to the police where Greenpeace was the subject of those emails … The police refused to release the information on the basis that there was too much of it. They said just looking at a single email address showed many hundreds of emails that met that search criteria. (Quoted in Penfold and Bingham 2018)

This suggests complex entanglements between the NZ Police, the oil and gas industry, and Thompson and Clark.

In March 2018, emails between the ministry responsible for regulating the oil and gas sector (the Ministry for Business, Innovation and Employment or MBIE) and Thompson and Clark were released to Oil Free Wellington under an OIA request. These emails showed that Thompson and Clark had 'watched' the group (*RNZ* 2018). MBIE had hired the security firm in 2013 to give advice in advance of protests at an annually held Petroleum Conference, a site of regular climate justice activism by numerous groups, including those in our study. MBIE denied hiring them since that time. There were, however, regular briefings about activist groups supplied by Thompson and Clark to the ministry in the years after. The ministry described this communication as newsletters that didn't contain the personal information of activists (Hobbs 2018). Thompson and Clark also initiated a group – Taranaki Oil and Gas Security Working Group – that involved oil companies, including Anadarko, OMV and NZ Oil and Gas, along with representatives of government departments, the police and MBIE. It is difficult to find information on this forum, but reporting on documents released under the OIA indicate that it was formed to discuss security matters and had at least one meeting, held in 'the bunker', the secure national crisis management centre under one of the Parliament buildings (Bingham and Penfold 2018).

Further surveillance tactics are evident in periods just prior to various direct actions that targeted the oil and gas industry, which coincided with spikes in requests for motor vehicle registration information (Hobbs 2018). Vehicle registration information requests involve submitting a licence plate number and sending a request to the licensing agency for owner information. This information, including the address of the car owner, is available only to certain groups like car dealers, police and private investigators. One media organisation's analysis of these requests showed higher requests when the Greenpeace vessel the *Rainbow Warrior* visited Aotearoa New Zealand in 2013, and again when oil company Anadarko's ships were active in New Zealand waters in 2014 (Hobbs 2018).

Many of these surveillance practices are in keeping with some of the more sinister actions of the PR industry as they become more often engaged in 'crisis management', as occurred when the scientific link between cancer and tobacco emerged. Other tactics include managing media and creating 'front groups' as a voice of 'reason' but promoting misinformation (see Monbiot 2007; Stauber and Rampton 1995), and using these and the media to 'manufacture consent' on the continuance of the industry in question (Chomsky and Herman 1994).

The findings of Greenpeace's investigation received little public attention. This is possibly because of the persistent erosion of the legitimacy of activism around the same time. As we described in Chapter 4, activists were often portrayed as 'others and outcasts' (Massaro and Williams 2013) through statements from national leaders and reporting by the media.

However, the public response, and media reporting, took a different tone when in March 2018 it emerged that Thompson and Clark had been spying on earthquake insurance claimants in Canterbury on the east coast of the South Island. The targeted claimants were challenging the decisions of state-owned insurance provider Southern Response. A series of large earthquakes in the city of Ōtautahi Christchurch and the surrounding Canterbury region killed 181 people in February 2011, and made thousands of people homeless. The earthquakes led to a flood of insurance claims, and ongoing contestation (over ten years later) over the way many of them were handled. A number of revelations quickly followed on various government ministries and agencies who were also using Thompson and Clark, although it wasn't always clear what they were used for. These government ministries and agencies included the Police, Department of Conservation, the Ministry of Primary Industries, the Ministry of Health and the Ministry of Foreign Affairs and Trade (see Edwards 2018; Fleming 2018a, 2018b; Penfold and Bingham 2018).

The surprising number of government departments using Thompson and Clark reflects an increased perception that certain individuals are a threat or present a risk to government operations (*Otago Daily Times* 2018). This may be linked to an event in 2014, where a client of Work and Income New Zealand (the social support agency that manages access to benefits and living supplements) took a shotgun into his local branch in a small South Island town, and murdered two women who worked there. In the wake of this event, government departments were required to develop 'Protective Security Requirements' (PSR). These plans involve identifying and mitigating risk in a 'diverse and complex threat landscape' (Protective Security, n.d.) and have created a new area for private profit by companies like Thompson and Clark (*NZ Herald* 2018).

Nevertheless, the revelations in 2018 prompted an official inquiry into all public agency connections with Thompson and Clark by the State Services Commission (an agency that monitors all government services and agencies to ensure they meet standards within their code of conduct[1]). The inquiry team issued a report in December 2018 that cleared many agencies concerned of any serious breach of their code of conduct (Martin and Mount 2018). However, it also reported on a number of worrying relationships between agencies and private security companies and undemocratic practices. Some of these related to the oil and gas industry and associated state agencies where there was a breach of the code of conduct's expectations of impartiality, trustworthiness, fairness and responsibility. In particular, the inquiry found that the branch of MBIE that is tasked with both promoting oil and gas exploration and regulating the industry sometimes 'lacked the impartiality, objectivity and professional distance' required by the code of conduct in their dealings with Thompson and Clark (Martin and Mount 2018, p. 64).

In the State Services Commission Inquiry, the proximity of some relationships between government agencies and Thompson and Clark was contrasted with the absence of any relationship with civil society and environmental groups. The Inquiry suggested that this neglected state agencies' responsibility to engage with and consider the full range of perspectives and interests (Martin and Mount 2018, p. 66). Further, the Inquiry was scathing of the way government agencies adopted Thompson and Clark's framing of groups as 'issue motivated groups'. This language originates with intelligence and risk management communities (Martin and Mount 2018), and was applied to community climate justice groups, Greenpeace, some iwi and the Green Party, among others. The Inquiry further suggested that in their newsletters, which were distributed regularly to MBIE, Thompson and Clark may have taken the views of individuals with 'more extreme' views, and portrayed them as the whole groups' perspective to justify characterising 'issue motivated groups' as security threats (Martin and Mount 2018, p. 70). This can, the Inquiry reported, lead to an overstatement of risk. In light of the context of protective security requirements and the 'complex threat landscape', this portrayal risks legitimising further surveillance activities.

Tracing the exact relationships between the private oil and gas sector, and the surveillance they commissioned from Thompson and Clark is more difficult than finding out about the state's entanglements with the PR firm. The private sector is not subject to the Official Information Act reporting requirements and expectations around transparency. However, the Inquiry stated that it was clear that 'Thompson and Clark has undertaken significant and sustained surveillance of Greenpeace, most likely paid for by private-sector petroleum and minerals interests' (Martin and Mount 2018, p. 66). The security company described working for the oil and gas sector from around 2012, and Hager (2021) quotes them as saying '[w]e have provided threat, risk assessment and security planning for each year's operation on behalf of our clients.... [against] a highly organised and motivated threat'. At some points, OMV were receiving daily briefings from Thompson and Clark as they monitored activists' plans through social media, and sought to undermine any action by issuing trespass notices and liaising with police (Hager 2021). Police engaged in their own surveillance of activists – turning up at people's homes unexpectedly, or through the extensive use of police photographers at protest events. The role of policing more broadly will be discussed in the next chapter.

EMBODYING SURVEILLANCE

While surveillance in and of itself is not inherently bad (as noted above, Lyon [2001] gives the example of caring by keeping an eye on someone), surveillance by private companies and its influence on the public sector has been borne out of *and* has created a climate of fear. This fear is designed to manage and control those who dissent against business-as-usual and constrain activities that highlight the social and environmental harms of industry in order to maintain its profit-making status. This climate of fear makes democratic activities – contesting insurance claims via the courts through to direct action against polluting industries – higher stakes. Naomi Klein (2002, p. 8) writes that through surveillance, companies go against key democratic principles of engaging in debate and disagreement and instead attempt to 'contain, intimidate and ultimately eliminate the opposition'. In a prominent example of surveillance and its pressure on democracy in Aotearoa New Zealand, French spies planted two bombs on the *Rainbow Warrior* in Auckland Harbour in 1985, killing one person, Fernando Pereira. The Greenpeace ship was about to lead a flotilla against nuclear testing in French Polynesia.

Frances Mountier (2018), a climate justice activist who has been involved in two groups targeted by Thompson and Clark wrote:

> The danger of Thompson and Clark is that its whole business model is working to stop democracy, to curtail citizens' rights to have meaningful input in the political sphere. Fundamentally they aim to delegitimise, stigmatise and criminalise people who are exercising their freedom of speech.

Talking about previous instances of spying on environmental and Indigenous sovereignty groups, one interviewee said 'I think the biggest damage that Thompson and Clark did us was that they made us stop trusting each other … we were paralysed by our own fear' (interview with Vicki). After their experiences of infiltration, people questioned their relationships with others, and were suddenly aware of being watched and regulated their actions accordingly. Similarly, the Director of Greenpeace reported that staff felt frightened by surveillance: 'Staff are feeling nervous on their way to work, and now have to check over their shoulder wherever they go' (Norman, cited in Taylor 2017).

Roznawska (2019, p. 30) argues that legal accountability mechanisms for infiltration and surveillance is of 'limited effectiveness'. And so one response by groups was to engage in their own practices of securitisation. For instance, Greenpeace's initial revelations about Thompson and Clark spying on them were supported with information from their own counter-surveillance where Greenpeace staff recorded vehicle details when they were being tailed (Taylor 2017). Similarly, a member of one Oil Free group described their own 'security culture', creating processes to secure against infiltration:

> Oil Free has a very specific policy about new members of the group ... which is partly about a security culture and in talking about actions, we're not *super* security conscious but we're security conscious. (Interview with Flo)

Similarly, another group sought a balanced approach when asked explicitly about how surveillance was managed within the group:

> Gradon: So within the Oil Free group, have you guys talked about the threats of police surveillance and protecting yourselves and how you communicate, that kind of thing?
>
> Dougie: Yeah. Yeah, yeah. To support each other and our people ... I suppose so that they don't inadvertently, you know, give information away. And I suppose becoming a lot more aware of our rights ... without becoming paranoid, yeah. (Interview with Dougie)

These participants described developing new policies and practices for new members – finding out about who they are but also supporting them to be careful with information and know their rights. These practices are entwined with a feminist ethic of care (discussed further in Chapter 7) – as a more care-full practice of internal surveillance in which care is a shared endeavour of looking out for each other in the groups. Such practices are particularly important as groups negotiate issues of climate justice that are underpinned by care for others (human and more than human).

CONCLUSION

While our whole project has been framed within feminist political geographies (as discussed in Chapter 1), this chapter in particular uses it to draw attention to the process by which the state adjudicates who is and who is not entitled to receive state help (even when contracted to private firms) to produce security (Hyndman 2007). While Hansen and Uldham (2015) argue that corporate surveillance has taken hold because state roles have been diminished by neoliberalism (discussed in Chapter 2), our case study and approach demonstrate that the state played a central role in enabling and normalising the surveillance of activists. Across a number of state agencies, a private security company was hired to assess risk and watch people. In relation to climate activists, the communication between the police and Thompson and Clark, who were conducting much of the surveillance, was so extensive that there was too much to compile in order to release under the OIA request. The close relationships between state agencies and Thompson and Clark, acting on behalf of the oil and gas industry, sought to produce security and certainty for fossil fuel interests, and insecurity for climate activists and civil society more generally.

In keeping with feminist geopolitics, we see that the current intersections of state and the private sector in surveilling communities and activists produces injustice. While the people we spoke with during our research had developed coping mechanisms to mitigate the fear and uncertainty of surveillance, it is clear that targeting activists has implications for democracy. Surveillance was, at times, compounded by policing practices that further dehumanised activists. While some violent policing practices were discussed in relation to the ANZ action in Chapter 4, the next chapter picks up on these and further examples.

6

Policing and Dehumanising Activists

Policing in Western countries is a particular form of securitisation, one that is often oriented towards (a version of) public safety and order. The relationship between policing and protest is often fraught, and run through with violent interactions that are able to happen because of the dehumanisation of activists. In this chapter, we explore contemporary policing of climate activists in Western democracies; focusing on who is subjected to violence, a particularly important concern in (post)colonial contexts. This policing isn't as violent or deadly as pro-extractive policing in many other parts of the world. All the same, the way police violence undermines environmental democracy requires careful attention.

In 2020, the New Zealand Police (who do not generally carry arms) completed a trial of roaming armed police units which were mostly based in majority Māori and Pasifika communities (Rākete 2020). In the same year, widespread protests and riots erupted again in the US in the wake of the police killing of George Floyd. In response to both contexts, abolitionist groups (groups calling for the abolition of prisons and a wholesale restructuring of Western-style justice systems) are calling for police to be de-funded because they have failed to keep Indigenous people and people of colour safe. More than that, the justice system represents a direct threat to these communities. Abolitionist groups argue that funding could be poured into initiatives, like secure housing, that prevent crime in the first instance (see People Against Prisons Aotearoa 2016), and into providing well-trained mental health workers and community responders for when prevention hasn't worked.

In contrast, police and others argue that in the past 40 years, policing in Western countries has changed and is increasingly done by community consent, with a significant emphasis on de-escalation and peace-keeping (for an overview of these arguments, see Loftus 2010). This community-oriented approach has tended to focus on crime prevention and building positive police/public relationships through a more diverse police force. Loftus (2010), writing in a UK context, argues however that the features underpinning police culture have not changed. Rank and file officers continue to reproduce cultures of masculine workplaces that seek danger and excitement, that are suspicious and defensive towards the public, and are based on simplistic understandings of criminality and a defensive commitment to the status quo. Focusing on youth-led protest in Britain, Pickard (2019) argues that policing has actually become more oppressive and militaristic. She describes the increasing police access to equipment like water cannons and tasers, increased surveillance of activists, use of pepper sprays and tear gas (also see Feigenbaum 2017), and practices like pre-emptive policing, containment (e.g. kettling) and mass arrests that have become more prevalent in recent years. When it comes to policing protest, the risks of a militarised police culture are apparent. In 2019, anti-extractivism activists blockaded a Melbourne mining conference. The police response was brutal, with activists and journalists pushed and pepper sprayed (Australian Associated Press 2019), and one police officer investigated for displaying iconography associated with white supremacy groups. In recent protests in the US, people have lost eyes and experienced frontal lobe brain injuries due to police use of 'less lethal' weapons (Schwartz 2020).

Public licence for this style of policing – where it does exist – may be partly driven by changing discourses around environmental activism that frame groups as terroristic, or pre-terroristic. As we have described in Chapter 3, in liberal democracies everywhere, there are increasingly authoritarian attitudes and punitive legislative tools that criminalise protest and normalise surveillance. These laws expand police powers to interfere with what many people think of as their democratic rights to voice, dissent and action. But Brock (2020) argues that police themselves take an active, highly politicised role in determining what counts as terrorism. Terrorism is by definition, an intent to induce terror and fear in society through a threat of, or actual violence. And yet, in the UK in 2019, XR, who explicitly embrace non-violent direct action and civil disobedience, was placed on a list of extremist groups curated by UK counter-terrorism police. The listing was part of the PREVENT programme, aimed at stopping ideological extremism, both far left and far right (Dodd and Greirson 2020). Police advice about extremism has led to intelligence gathering about people opposing fossil fuels and anti-fracking activists, including children (Brock 2020). Here, the definition of terrorism is extended beyond common sense to enable the expansion of police powers, to criminalise protest, normalise surveillance and maintain social norms that delegitimise dissent.

Surveillance and to a degree infiltration were discussed in the previous chapter, but it's worth noting the way that police infiltration acts as a pre-emptive form of securitisation that tries to quash dissent. In recent years, there have been numerous revelations of police infiltration of activist groups in the UK, to the point that undercover officers entered long-standing relationships with their subjects and in some instances had children with them. The revelations prompted the UK government to launch an inquiry in 2015 to investigate undercover policing in England and Wales stretching back to the 1960s (Undercover Policing Inquiry n.d.). The inquiry is due to release findings in 2023.

Disclosures of police infiltration and spying have been harder to trace in our case study in Aotearoa New Zealand. Therefore, the previous chapter explored surveillance with a focus on private companies, sometimes at the behest of state agencies. We think there is likely to be ongoing police infiltration of environmental activist groups here, just as there has been in the past (for instance, see Morse 2019a) but this chapter focuses on public policing of activists, particularly at protests. Further, Brock (2020) demonstrates the increasingly blurry relationships that constitute 'policing' of resistance to fracking in the UK. She argues that it is made up of uniformed police, security companies, undercover police, and people working for state agencies that exact punishments on activists. In what follows we highlight how policing practices have developed in Aotearoa New Zealand and have targeted climate justice activists in different contexts.

POLICING PROTEST AND COLONIALISM

Aotearoa New Zealand's police force emerged out of the armed constabulary that was formed in the late 1800s to help roll out violent colonisation. From the beginnings of colonisation, there was widespread protest and resistance by Māori to land confiscations, dodgy 'sales' and unfulfilled promises by the Crown. This conflict is often represented through one of the most prominent confrontations of the 1800s. The community at Parihaka, in Taranaki on the west coast of the North Island, had become a place where Māori who had been dispossessed of their land gathered and adopted principles of non-violent resistance as they sought a safe space within context of escalating violence against them. In 1881, the Armed

Constabulary (a mix of police and military) and volunteers invaded Parihaka by order of the governor, arrested leaders, destroyed much of the settlement, committed assaults and rape, and dispersed 1,600 people from the settlement. Two years after the invasion, the Police was created out of the Armed Constabulary.

More than a hundred years later, the Waitangi Tribunal (1996, p. 199) noted the ongoing significance of Parihaka in Aotearoa New Zealand:

> Parihaka is symbolic of autonomy – of the right of Indigenous peoples to maintain their society on their own terms and to develop, from mutual respect, a peaceful relationship and partnership with the government.

Nevertheless, the strands of violent policing of protest have remained with the police force. These strands were evident in the policing of the labour movement in the 1910s, and the 1950 wharf strikes, but have remained particularly pronounced when it comes to policing Māori.

It takes constant work to maintain the colonial state and white possessiveness of Indigenous places. For instance, Takaparawhau (Bastion Point) was a site of contestation in Tāmaki Makaurau Auckland since the mid-1800s. Through a series of actions by the government and Native Land Court, tangata whenua (Māori tied to that place) were alienated from their land and the Treaty was breached. In the 1970s, in response to government plans to develop housing on Takaparawhau, members of Ngāti Whātua Ōrakei led 506 days of protest whereby people moved onto the land and built gardens and accommodation. This was during the broader Māori land rights movement during the 1970s (discussed in Chapter 2). The protest was brought to an end on 25 May 1978 when police and the army evicted the people at the site and arrested 222 people for trespassing. This use of the military in policing assertions of sovereignty foreshadows the arrest of Elvis Teddy, skipper of Te Whānau-ā-Apanui's vessel, in 2011 in the Raukūmara Basin (see Chapter 3).

In Aotearoa New Zealand, operational policing and the justice system has been, in principle, independent of the government (Roznawska 2019) as part of the separation of powers that enables checks and balances to occur in a functional democracy. In reality, however, this independence has not been consistent, and is questionable when police violence, particularly against Indigenous sovereignty movements, can be read as one example of 'state sovereignty [being] articulated through on-going acts of violent legitimation' (Aikman 2017, p. 59). In the wake of 9/11, Aotearoa New Zealand introduced anti-terror legislation and there was a burgeoning of terror discourses. In particular, the terror threat was framed as coming from Māori sovereignty activists, culminating in raids in 2007 on activist communities and a palpable targeting of the Tūhoe nation in the central North Island. Maria Bargh (2012, p. 128) writes that the raids 'highlighted the high levels of state surveillance of those who seek to challenge or even critique its authority'. Furthermore, these raids and the justification for enacting them framed activists' behaviour as pre-terroristic, 'invested with the potential for future harm' (Wakeham 2012, p. 12). While it's important to be clear that the policing of Indigenous people, and of sovereignty movements, have a long and often different history to the policing of environmental and social justice activists more broadly (Stewart-Harawira 2008), they share a normalisation of fear, othering and accusations of terrorism (see, for example, Humphreys 2009; Locke 2019). Importantly, contestation of fossil fuels is often the context that brings to the fore Indigenous struggles for sovereignty.

For instance, in Canada, some members of the Wet'suwet'en nation mobilised to block a gas pipeline across their territory. In earlier decades, judicial processes that recognised aboriginal title had been viewed by the fossil fuel industry as a threat to operations, and the Canadian government worried about Indigenous land rights undermining Canada's business friendliness for that industry (Brown and Bracken 2020). As confrontation escalated throughout the 2010s, documents leaked in early 2020 showed that Royal Canadian Mounted Police commanders argued for the deployment of officers prepared to use lethal force against Indigenous people. Other officers argued for arrests in order to 'sterilize' the site (Dhillon and Parrish 2019). Rather than these sorts of framings being out of the ordinary though, Aikman (2017, p. 69) argues that they are entirely normal, and therefore the instance of the 2007 Tūhoe raids was 'not exceptional, but routine functions of the settler colonial state'.

For many people across the world, police violence is a familiar and regular occurrence, and there has been significant work demonstrating how certain groups of people experience both police and publicly sanctioned violence much more than others. In a global review of environmental activism, Scheidel et al. (2020) found that Indigenous people experience higher rates of violence. In focusing on Western democracies, we are missing a large part of the story of policing of environmental activism. As Glazebrook and Okopu (2018) describe, collusion between states (including police) and global capital have been deadly for many environmental activists. After describing murders in Latin America, the Philippines and India, they write:

> None of these protectors were murdered in the global North, though the industries that defenders defend against are usually financed in large part by multinationals with head offices in the global North. That is to say, the global South remains deeply entangled in post-colonial economics of resource exploitation. (Glazebrook and Okupu 2018, p. 86)

These uneven policing practices illustrates a deeper issue according to Judith Butler (2004, p. 91): 'the question of who will be treated humanely presupposes that we have first settled the question of who does and does not count as a human'. It's not enough to say that the unevenness of these practices globally is relative to their context. These policing practices are part of a wider entangled global system with local effects. While extractive industries and fossil fuels may be the provocation that leads to confrontation and public conflict, they are often just the backdrop to deeper political claims that relate to sovereignty and power and reflect existing societal divisions. Contestation related to sovereignty represents a profound threat to the state, which combined with institutionalised racism, perhaps accounts for the far-reaching, often violent, reactions by police forces and state spy agencies to Indigenous movements.

CONSENT AND FORCE IN AOTEAROA NEW ZEALAND

Like other Western democracies, police in Aotearoa New Zealand have focused their narratives on community policing and policing by consent in recent decades (see, for instance, Coster 2020). These narratives seemingly promise a shift away from repressive or violent modes of societal control. This narrative has been troubled at key moments, such as debates about whether to routinely arm police with tasers (which they were in 2015), and the 2019 to 2020 trial of roaming armed police units mentioned above, which the police backed away from under intense community backlash. In 2021, there were renewed calls to routinely arm the police; Aotearoa New Zealand is one of just a few jurisdictions where police do not carry firearms with them. Instead, they are stored and locked in vehicles. Police are empowered to use force under the Crimes

Act 1961, but what is meant by 'reasonable force' and the circumstances under which it is allowed are not clearly spelled out (Wainsbrough 2008). And, despite not routinely carrying arms, New Zealand police killed citizens at eleven times the rate of England and Wales police since 1990 (Hancock and Espiner 2022). Furthermore, in contradiction to policing by consent, resources put into breaking blockades at peace and climate justice actions grew significantly in the years of our study. For instance, the police spent NZD186,000 on securing an annual oil and gas industry conference in 2018 (Stewart 2018). This is an increase in spending of $70,000 from policing a similar sized, peace-focused blockade in 2017, and an increase of $160,000 from that same peace blockade in 2015. These same events are sometimes followed by pernicious police prosecutions of activists. For instance, after the 2015 peace blockade of a weapons expo, charges were brought against 16 activists for trespass and obstruction. These charges were later dropped as the activists were on public land. But the time, cost and stress of being taken through the legal process to that point was significant and may have a deterrent effect. The spokesperson for Peace Action Wellington said 'They've charged us to stop us from doing it again ... People don't want to go to court – we had to take a week off work' (quoted in Irwin 2017). The number of activists, and especially activists involved in organising campaigns, in Aotearoa New Zealand is small. Peace and climate justice activists are often the same people. So the same people, who see and confront the overlapping concerns of colonisation, nationalism, militarisation, and capitalism, are targeted by pernicious police prosecutions and intensive policing practices.

A MONOPOLY ON VIOLENCE: ŌTEPOTI DUNEDIN AND TE WHANGANUI-A-TARA WELLINGTON

As a research team wanting to deeply understand the Oil Free and climate justice movements, we were often present at actions and events. The three of us engage differently with scholar activism in ways that reflect our contexts, shaped by how we're each able to have efficacy, what our different skills are, and the differing responsibilities and connections we have within our communities. In this sense, we are influenced by generations of feminist geographers who have drawn attention to the politics of knowledge (Hiemstra and Billo 2017; Noxolo, Raghuram and Madge 2012; Raghuram, Madge and Noxolo 2009; Sharp 2009; Wright 2009), and critical geographers who mix thinking with doing to build just futures (Askins and Swanson 2019; Chatterton, Hodkinson and Pickerill 2010; Pain, Kesby and Askins 2011; Routledge 2017). At various stages we've engaged in protest, helped to lead protest briefings and debriefings, joined banner making, and worked with others to organise blockades. In more confrontational actions, we have all witnessed aggressive action by police.

In Chapter 4 we described how activists blockaded ANZ bank branches in Ōtepoti Dunedin in 2016, and the violent response from police and members of the public. While some activists had anticipated being arrested, or physically removed from the blockade by police, they had not anticipated being assaulted by the police, or members of the public who were encouraged by the police to use 'reasonable force' to get through the blockade to access the ANZ branches. What happened reflected media and police portrayals of protestors that often emphasise deviance and a 'just deserts' public response (Diprose et al. 2017).

Activists described how they were shoved, kneed, punched, kicked, stomped on, walked over and verbally abused by members of the public and police. For example, George reported that 'one of the cops, without any indication, just kneed me straight in the back, and drilled me into the ground, my head was like going into the door' (interview with George). The police were saying to people 'just stand on them' (interview with Frankie). Another described how:

one guy who ran through and like kicked a girl on the way in, and then everyone who was being let in, like through us, was being told to leave [the branch] by the side door, but then he decided to come back without any warning, and came through right fast and kicked this girl in the back of the head, and then … he said something horrible, and like the cops [were] just standing right there. (Interview with George)

For some activists, who were perhaps new to activism, these police actions were unsettling and surprising. In their view, the role of the police in society was about protecting people and de-escalating violence or conflict, not provoking or enabling it, in line with the core values promoted by the New Zealand Police around community safety and security. However, the experience of the action changed this significantly for several activists. It highlighted how fragile social harmony is, and how quickly some people can be urged into violence, or a 'rage' when authorised to do so by those in authority.

These activists' experiences of surprise contrast with those from many Māori and Pasifika communities, both of which have long experienced police violence and public 'rage'. We have described the colonial roots of policing above, and numerous reports in recent decades have highlighted the persistent racism within the police (see, for instance, Te Whaiti and Roguski 1998). For Pasifika people, there is also the long shadow of the dawn raids of the 1970s, when the Pacific community was scapegoated by the New Zealand public for a flagging economy, violently policed and many of its members deported (Allen and Bruce 2017; Anae et al. 2015; Anae 2020).

For some of the activists we spoke to, this was their first experience of both direct action and contesting more dominant power relations in their community. Some described feeling dehumanised, as 'objects' to inflict pain on (interview with Rachel). Others described how when someone hurts your body 'it's kind of them saying ... we're not regarding you ... as a being that's ... experiencing this pain' (interview with Sal). Returning to the quote above by Judith Butler, in which she raises the question of violence and what it shows in terms of who 'counts as human', it is clear that those who were violent toward the activists did so because they were able to dehumanise the activists through their framing of them (Butler 2004). In the ANZ protest, the way in which the police endorsed and authorised members of the public to be violent toward protestors reflected a social order in which the activists' bodies (and message) did not count. This, combined with the complicity of the state in criminalising protest at sea (discussed in Chapter 3), alongside the kinds of media portrayals of 'hippies' and 'hypocrites' designed to delegitimise activists (discussed in Chapter 4) demonstrate the extent of already existing social norms that close down democratic debate when the status quo is put into question.

Reflecting the events in Ōtepoti Dunedin, in another example, the annual Petroleum Industry conference in Aotearoa New Zealand has been a consistent site of confrontation and protest. In recent years, it has been held in Ngāmotu New Plymouth, Tāmaki Makaurau Auckland and, in March 2018, in Te Whanganui-a-Tara Wellington. That year, the police arrived at the conference venue at 5.30 a.m., marching through the dark to facilitate conference attendees' entry to the building from around 6 a.m. onwards. The venue had multiple doors and around 200 activists were spread thinly trying to block access from 5 a.m. (Williams, Cann and Rutherford 2018). Police were incredibly rough with people. People were shoved, grabbed by the throat, pushed over, verbally threatened, and one person had their head smashed into concrete and had to be taken to hospital. Activists persisted until around 1.30 p.m., by which time most conference delegates were inside, and the focus had shifted to noise disruption. Debriefing at the end of the day, many were visibly shocked by the police actions, wondering aloud what had been done to provoke them as that was the only rationale they could imagine for that kind of treatment. Culturally, there is a high value placed on social cohesion and homogeneity in Aotearoa New Zealand. As we discussed in Chapter 4, there is often intolerance of people that disrupt or challenge the status quo. Roznawska (2019) argues that these attitudes contribute to a 'culture of security'; public responses to extreme policing emphasise that the targets must have, somehow, 'deserved it'. Pākehā in particular have internalised this narrative, so like the ANZ actions in Ōtepoti Dunedin mentioned above, blockading the petroleum conference was for many their first experience of police violence. Through this exposure, they were forced to reckon with assumptions about who 'deserved' violence.

A MONOPOLY ON VIOLENCE: POLICE ACCOUNTABILITY

In Aotearoa New Zealand, complaints about the police are handled by the Independent Police Conduct Authority (IPCA), which promises to be independent in their review of complaints. The IPCA was established after the police violence during protests against the Springbok rugby tour in 1981, specifically in response to unease about police tactics and a lack of accountability. That year, the South African rugby team, the Springboks, toured Aotearoa New Zealand, despite enormous international (and growing domestic) pressure to sever sporting contacts due to apartheid. The anti-tour movement organised more than 200 demonstrations, and involved 150,000 people. Roche writes that, in response, 'a third to a half of the police force [were] involved in ensuring test matches could proceed' (Roche 1997, p. 52, drawing on Trevor Richards 1996). The police were decked out in visors and shields with long batons, and conducted baton charges against protestors, the first time this had been done in 30 years (Roche 1997). Complaints against the police, at that time, were investigated internally. Dissatisfaction with this led to a Police Complaints Authority being established in 1989 to try to establish some distance. The independence of the Authority was intensely questioned in the following two decades however, particularly by Māori and people who had been sexually assaulted by police. The Authority didn't have its own investigators independent of the police until 2003 (Espiner 2022). In 2007, the Authority was overhauled and became the Independent Police Conduct Authority (IPCA). Other than cases involving death or serious injury, the IPCA investigates police actions only in response to complaints, and even then, only conducts their own independent investigation into 2 per cent of complaints (Espiner 2022). In the remaining 98 per cent, the police investigate themselves or complaints aren't acted on. The IPCA's responsive position means they cannot be proactive in changing racist or discriminatory work culture and practices, and can only make recommendations, that may then be ignored.

After the 2018 petroleum conference, a number of people complained to the IPCA, including Amanda. During the course of the blockade, she was part of a group obstructing a door at the event centre. Amanda's version of scholar activism draws on traditions of direct activism that intervene in the institutions and processes that generate injustice. In this instance, blockading the petroleum conference was one way of intervening in some of the processes exacerbating climate change. During the blockade, there were waves of confrontation with the police as they tried to get conference attendees into the venue through different doors. The confrontations were typified by the police heavy-handedness described above. At one point, Amanda was shoved from behind and tripped over two protestors who had been pushed to the ground by police. As she fell, she grabbed at something to steady herself, and realised that she had gripped a police officer's rain jacket. Another officer saw this and said 'touch him again, and I'll fucking knock you out'. This threat was the basis of a complaint to the IPCA. The officer's response to the complaint was that Amanda had simply misheard and that he actually said 'touch him again and I'm gunna lock you up'. In the response by the IPCA to Amanda's complaint, they wrote:

> The Police sergeant denies threatening you with violence and it is apparent from his statement that he believes you misheard his comment amid the surrounding noise of the protest. After reviewing all of the available information the Authority has therefore been provided with conflicting accounts regarding your complaint about the attitude and language of the Police sergeant during this incident. It is unlikely that

any further enquiries would be able to resolve this conflict between the accounts. (IPCA letter 2018)

The letter stated that both accounts were credible and without further information they were 'unable to uphold [the] complaint'. The importance of this needs to be understood in the context of a police monopoly on violence. Roznawska states that 'when it comes to matters of police conduct, the public good (determined by politically sanctioned cultural values of the moment) takes priority over democratic values. We delegate a wide discretion to the police and resist holding them accountable' (2019, p. 47). The IPCA, in its decision that conflicting accounts meant they couldn't uphold the complaint, expands police discretionary powers and reinforces this unevenness when it comes to how to engage with conflict. This is, of course, an obvious point – the police are able to restrain and handle people in a way that, if someone reciprocated, they would likely face quite serious consequences in the criminal justice system. But when the deciding factor – in relation to protest – is that there are differing accounts, all it takes for the police to avoid consequences for abusing their monopoly on violence is to offer a different account of what happened.

Not only do police have a very wide scope to determine what counts as reasonable force and legitimate police violence (see also Jackson 2020), they decide who counts as human. In the case of the Ōtepoti Dunedin protest, activists had been delegitimised and undermined to the point that other members of the public felt emboldened through the permission of the police to use reasonable force. Moreover, this monopoly has added significance in relation to the institutionalised racism of police forces. Police are seven times more likely to use force against Māori compared to Pākehā (Neilson 2020).

The treatment of Oil Free and climate activists contrasts starkly with a 2022 occupation of Parliament lawns by anti-vaccine mandate protestors, anti-vaxxers, far-right groups and other people drawn in by misogyny, white supremacy, far-right free speech narratives, or a deep distrust of the colonial state (Daalder 2022). For three weeks, hundreds of people camped outside Parliament, blockaded streets and disrupted schools and businesses. The protest ended in a fiery confrontation between police and the protesters, but prior to that, obvious threats of violence, particularly against politicians and media, and frequent abuse of people walking by wearing masks, were not responded to by police. For many climate activists who had engaged in non-violent direct action and experienced police violence, the contrasting treatment was galling.

How then can the public have accountability, particularly when the police have a monopoly on violence? Eveline Lubbers (2019) describes the extensive work by activist networks to research, expose and seek accountability for police and private security infiltration into activist groups. It was through the persistence of activists, for instance, that groups were able to expose decades of police infiltration, involving more than one hundred officers, and subversion of political groups in Britain (Lubbers 2019). Citizen surveillance of police might also take the form of videoing and recording encounters, like the actions of Darnella Frazier, who filmed the murder of George Floyd by police in Minneapolis. Or another example would be the handful of blockaders at the Wellington petroleum industry conference who were tasked with filming the day so that instances of police violence could be captured or pernicious prosecutions countered. While the pervasiveness of surveillance – from data harvesting to cityscapes filled with security cameras – often represents a threat to activists challenging the status quo, the democratisation of surveillance technologies is an important counter to police violence. Sustaining this kind of work also requires environmental groups to build alliances with justice and abolitionist activist groups who work to counter the use of police force and the highly racialised nature of it.

CONCLUSION

We described in earlier chapters the shifting legislative frameworks that herald more authoritarian responses to protest in Western democracies. In this chapter, we have described the role of police enforcing such legislative provisions, but also in shaping the terrain of who is seen to be a threat. In (post)colonial contexts like Aotearoa New Zealand, the roots of police are in the forces that violently dispossessed Indigenous people of land. These roots have revealed themselves over and over through the policing of Māori.

In contrast to Māori communities' experiences of policing and being constructed as 'threat' – which is nothing more or less than the ordinary functioning of the settler colonial state (Aikman 2017) – there is work to be done to challenge naive or overly positive views of the police in many environmental groups. Many young white people in these groups are raised to have a high degree of trust in the police as an institution, and the police narratives emphasising policing by consent. Communities of colour and Indigenous folks' accounts of violent policing and everyday dehumanisation are explained away or not believed. The lived experience, however, of the policing of oil and gas resistance has revealed the violence that is allowed and encouraged in the name of protecting the extractivist status quo. Police (and military) resources have been poured into the forceful policing of fossil fuel industry events, and prosecuting people like Elvis Teddy, skipper of the Te Whānau-ā-Apanui fishing boat (see Chapter 3). Furthermore, when people innocent to police violence encounter it in action, there can be unproductive self-blame amongst activists and an undermining of people's sense of agency.

The use of police resources to ensure the smooth operating of the fossil fuel industry demonstrates the close relationships between the state, the police as a part of the state, and the oil and gas industry. These relationships are made possible through neoliberal logics that rely on the state to create the conditions for privatised wealth accumulation, partly through disciplining deviant subjects. Through these decisions, police are reinforcing existing structural injustices that the neoliberal (post)colonial state rests upon. Therefore, in addition to conscientisation about the role of the police and considered discussion about the institutions past and future, there needs to be an urgent, fundamental shift in the role of the police in deciding who counts as humans, and who matters in their everyday operations.

Policing by force may represent a barrier to sustained politicisation for many people, like those activists targeted by pernicious prosecutions, or those accused of terrorism. However, for some people it also reveals the injustice of the system (Morse 2019a). Many of the people we spoke to reflected on the liberatory potential of direct action:

[It] really reinforced that actually civil disobedience is about overcoming your own conditioned obedience and your own conditioning to act in a way that's perceived as normal, or to act in a way that's perceived as socially acceptable and like all of these things which, actually we should be challenging, you know. I think like realising that civil disobedience isn't just about breaking those external laws. It's about trying to recognise when your own initial emotional or intellectual response needs to be disobeyed as well. (Interview with Sal)

7

Enacting Care and Responsibility

THE EMOTIONAL TOLL

So far, we've highlighted how neoliberalism and continuing forms of colonialism are anti-democratic in that they silence dissent through a range of tactics. These tactics are both enabled by and perpetuate the privileged roles of transnational corporations and governments. This involves government policies, regulations and legislation, mainstream and social media representations, forms of uneven and often violent policing and societal attitudes to activists who engage in radical actions. The previous chapters have documented a range of examples that demonstrate in many ways the *uncaring* and often violent nature of business-as-usual. These findings of a lack of care are supported by a number of scholars who suggest that this is prevalent because of neoliberalism's focus on the importance of individuals and the economy, combined with a tendency in Western thought to think of the environment or nature as a resource that is separate from humans (Brown 2015; Puig de la Bellascasa 2017; Tronto 2013; Winter 2020). So this carelessness is further compounded by the dominance of Western ways of knowing and thinking about the environment and people.

In the previous chapters we have also often extended the discussion beyond Aotearoa New Zealand's shores to demonstrate the widespread nature of these trends across liberal democracies. Our analysis has provided perspectives on climate and environmental activism that occurs in visible public spaces and through media. It has not yet considered the internal, personal, often difficult negotiations that activists engage in when they feel dehumanised by police or public violence as discussed in Chapters 4 and 6. Yet our conversations with activists reveal the emotional toll activism takes as they navigate everyday life. This internal personal struggle is significant and also works to silence dissent. For example, in our study on the Oil Free campaign in Aotearoa New Zealand, some participants, especially tertiary students, indicated that they feared what an arrest or their involvement in radical activist groups might look like on their CV as they were preparing to enter the workforce. Or they expressed concern that they might be recognised and discredited if social media or mainstream media revealed their engagement in activism. Another participant suggested involvement in non-violent direct action might compromise their chance of promotion, while others found they were increasingly isolated as they avoided people or places where disapproval of their activism was likely to be expressed. Still other participants referred to everyday interactions that included side glances, looks or comments from friends, family and colleagues that had a cumulative effect of delegitimising their activism. One commented that sometimes if felt like it wouldn't take much more than one more comment in the tea-room at work for them to go 'fuck it, I'm not going to do anything', referring to any further activism (see Bond, Thomas and Diprose 2020, p. 750).

While the effect of such comments and negotiations varied among activists, it suggests a societal level of carelessness around how activism is regarded, and by implication a carelessness for climate activism and climate justice. In this chapter we return to the ways that neoliberalism shapes the possibilities for meaningful change by arguing that carelessness is in part a result of the societal focus on individuals and individual responsibility (rather than collectives) that is a central characteristic of different forms of neoliberalism. We then move to explore how activists both in our study and in examples elsewhere have sought to subvert this pervasive lack of care by exercising care, by exploring the moral obligation many activists feel as they engage in this work collectively, and in the way that they assume and allocate responsibility for justice widely across society. We suggest that these caring spaces are radical spaces of action and change that offer hope.

CARELESSNESS IN NEOLIBERALISED SOCIETY

There are a number of ways that a lack of 'care' for the environment, the future, and for others is demonstrated in contemporary liberal democracies. In addition to silencing dissent against business-as-usual in the variety of ways we have described in preceding chapters, 'carelessness' also speaks to one reason why it is so difficult to get action on climate change. In turn, this lack of care generates a lack of, or misdirected, responsibility for climate change action. This section highlights four key dimensions of contemporary neoliberal capitalism that, we argue, reinforces this lack of care and irresponsibility.

First, contemporary liberal democracies and settler colonial societies have a long history of separating nature from human activities, and treating the natural environment as either a resource to extract, improve, or add value to and sell, or as a pollution 'sink' in which to flush away waste (Cronon 1996). Some argue that this in part comes from the influence of Christian thought over the ages, particularly in European and European colonial contexts, whereby humans are assumed to have mastery or dominion over the earth, rather than being subject to it or a part of it. This approach has been consolidated through the system of capitalism which holds a utilitarian approach to nature and natural environments. Others describe how humans are alienated from nature in a variety of ways under contemporary liberal capitalism. Referring to the work of Robert Cox, Morgan (2017) refers to alienation from the products of labour (knowing where goods come from), the labour process (who made them and how), from other humans (a lack of awareness of others' experiences and ways of being in the world especially those in less privileged positions), and finally alienation from understanding the ways that humans and human activities are embedded in ecological and earth system processes.

This last point in particular reflects a Western perspective, and we acknowledge that many Indigenous peoples are not alienated in these ways, and hold instead ways of being that tend to be more ecologically and otherwise embedded. Many radical and critical geographers have also highlighted this disconnect between nature and society as it is manifest in contemporary forms of capitalism (Bawaka Country et al. 2019; Castree and Braun 2001; Willems-Braun 1997; Winter 2020). When this disconnect is implicated in the alienations of both production and consumption processes discussed above, it becomes easier to understand how the kind of cognitive dissonance in relation to climate change occurs and is entrenched in societal norms, governance, institutions and knowledge.

One implication of the separation of nature and society is that while climate change is recognised as a growing international problem, it is not always or often associated with the need to fundamentally alter the capitalist system or the human relationship with nature that has generated the problem. This is so despite the broad consensus amongst scientists and many others that human activity and the use of fossil fuels since the industrial revolution is causing climate change beyond past natural variations. The global response to climate change and the efforts to mitigate greenhouse gases seems to suggest that it is possible to mitigate emissions through market mechanisms like carbon trading, without substantially altering business-as-usual. These efforts toward global mitigation both contribute to and reflect the disconnect between society and the natural environment. Carbon markets are a neoliberalised response that focuses on enabling markets to do the work of mitigation which chimes nicely with and maintains the ways in which nature and the impacts of capitalism on nature are distanced from human lives in dominant world views. In turn, this disconnect facilitates a way of thinking that means many people tend not to see their individual actions as contributing to climate change. Alternatively, it narrows the range of solutions available to address climate change to one that many people in their everyday lives cannot engage in, resulting in despair and uncertainty. In combination, these represent a number of distancing tactics – between nature and human activities, between climate change and everyday life, between mitigation and human behaviour, and between carbon markets and human action for change. Distancing generates a lack of care and an apparent carelessness about the environment.

Second, neoliberal practices, policies and forms of governing across society emphasise individuals over collectives. As noted in Chapter 2, neoliberalism developed as a counter-hegemonic project to Keynesianism, and the welfare state. It also pitched itself against paradigms of socialism and communism, and central interventions by the state toward a 'common' or collective good (Filip 2020). The argument put forward by early neoliberals such as Friedman and Hayek, as discussed in Chapter 2, was that the state had too much power to decide who or what should do what within the economy, that the state was the least efficient mechanism for allocating resources, and that such interventions in the economy hindered individual freedoms, especially in relation to private enterprise and property. Thus, neoliberals linked freedom with free individual economic choice. Again, this framing that emphasises individualism aligns with and reflects the disconnection between the individual and the wider collective common good, one of the alienations noted above between humans operating in society. The individualism inherent to a neoliberalised society therefore contributes to the continuation of a lack of care or a carelessness about the environment and other humans, further hindering efforts to address climate change in a meaningful way.

Third, and alongside the emphasis on individualism is what is sometimes called a responsibilisation discourse. Neoliberalism emphasises individuals' free choice, and so individuals are also seen to be responsible for their lot in life. For example, those in extreme poverty in liberal democracies are often blamed for making poor choices or failing to work hard enough to get themselves out of a poverty cycle. The assumption often espoused by neoliberals is that the playing field is level, and so, with hard work, grit and tenacity, anyone can succeed within a market-led system. This is based on an antiquated understanding of equality that many social theorists have debunked. Such a 'level playing field' approach fails to recognise that markets and free (economic) choices are far more accessible to those who already have resources (money, education, social connections, and so on) and that those resources are not readily available to everyone. They are typically less available to women, those with brown skin, or differently abled bodies, or those who do not identify as heterosexual and cis-gendered. As a result of this approach, individuals who do not succeed in the system tend to be deemed failures, or lazy. The effect of the emphasis on individuals over collectives, and associated responsibilisation is that it makes the broader system that creates inequalities and environmental degradation invisible. This is because the responsibility for performing well within society is placed on the individual, not on the system through which society operates.

Fourth, and rather ironically, such individualised responsibilisation discourses work against recognising who and what is responsible for climate change and mitigating or responding to its impacts. The very mechanisms that assume individuals are responsible for their socio-economic position arise because the individual is primary. Structural power relations (particularly those embedded through history like colonialism) and a deferral to the individual over the collective, means that the unequal impacts of climate change may be overlooked. Moreover, assuming individual responsibility for something that cannot be directly attributed to an individual's actions, especially in the context of human alienation from production and consumption processes, makes action on climate change doubly hard.

We have argued that a lack of care is evident in liberal democracies due to a Western world view that separates nature and society, emphasises individualism and responsibilisation and makes structural injustices invisible. The effect is to narrow down the possibilities for understanding who is responsible for addressing climate change and for caring about both the planet and those people who might be most affected by the impacts of a changing climate. Even for the many people who do articulate care, they are constantly challenged by these broader structural processes and the everyday busyness in which people are embedded. Many geographers and social theorists have referred to these as 'care deficits' that have arisen in relation to the expansion of neoliberal capitalism into all areas of society (Dowler et al. 2019; England 2010; Hochschild 2003; Lawson 2007; Tronto 2013). The corollary of a lack of care or 'care deficit' is that responsibility is also narrowly construed, which in turn also suggests a narrow understanding of how justice might be enacted.

IRRESPONSIBILITY AND INJUSTICE

Within liberal democracies, in which the justice system is a key part of governmental arrangements, justice has a particular common meaning. Iris Marion Young (2011) refers to this as a liability model of justice, where seeking justice involves attributing blame to a person (or to something with the status of a legal person like a company or a Council). Such an approach aligns neatly with neoliberal individualisation. Thus, responsibility within this framework is about identifying who is liable for a wrong, and how to recompense the 'victim' and secure just deserts such that the punishment is equal to the harm caused. Again, this liability model does not always reflect structural injustices or the nuanced ways that individuals and groups are forced into actions that would not be of their choosing if all else were equal (Ishiyama 2003).

Young (2011) also argues, that even for scholars and members of society that do recognise when harm or injustice occurs through no fault of any individual, that it is more about luck than any systemic dimension of society that anyone can do anything about it. As White (2018, p. 99) argues, even where:

[s]ystems are deemed to be blameworthy, ... they are not responsible insofar as there is no single 'controlling mind'. A system may be subjected to social and moral condemnation, but there is no single perpetrator as such. Yet, on reflection, we know that 'something is wrong' and that this occurs within the overarching parameters of global capitalism. The net result of this situation is systemic damage for which no one wants to claim responsibility, be held accountable or provide compensation.

Individualised neoliberal capitalism ignores the fact that societal structures that perpetuate injustices or environmental degradation come from somewhere. They evolve over time through the collective actions and decisions made by people. They are not inevitable, and nor are injustices that are caused by structural injustices a case of luck. They can be changed. Young (2011) argues that these views toward the individualisation and inevitability of injustice are the result of a lack of recognition of the ways everyday life are interconnected and interdependent. Because of the atomistic way in which people engage in everyday life, they tend not to recognise that their actions have an impact on others. She writes:

> The discourse of personal responsibility fails to acknowledge the many ways that some middle-class and rich people behave irresponsibly. It assumes a misleading ideal that each person can be independent of others and internalise the costs of their own actions. It ignores how the institutional relations in which we act render us deeply interdependent. The discourse fails to ask what personal responsibility individuals have for the conditions of the lives of others in these interdependent relationships, as well as for their own lives. (Young 2011, pp. 4–5)

Young is discussing these issues in the context of poverty in the US. She points out that those who are struggling in poverty are usually the target of policy initiatives to address poverty. For example, those in poverty may be directed to engage in other education opportunities, develop specific skills relevant to the employment market, live closer to where work is available that meets their skill sets. Often support is provided conditional on engaging in these kinds of activities. In relation to climate change the individualistic response is that people should reduce their emissions by changing their behaviour. But those in poverty may not be able to afford to do that, and have the least mobility in terms of moving away from areas where climate impacts are creating increased hazard risk like inundation or flooding. The attention is not on the transnational corporations who make others pay for the externalities their industries create, or the wealthy elite who evade taxes, or speculate in the housing market pushing house and rent prices up increasing the wealth gap, and who emit more through greater conspicuous consumption. Similar arguments might be made in relation to large corporations and high-emitting countries avoiding emissions reductions, in order to sustain the drive for economic growth, and privileged lifestyles. Akin to victim blaming, responsibility tends to be attributed to those who suffer the consequences, rather than those whose actions contribute to the harm, because the harm is not directly attributable to one person, but to whole populations and broader social, economic and political systems.

JUSTICE, RESPONSIBILITY AND CARE

Instead of an overly individualised, liability model of responsibility in which no one is responsible, or a single entity is targeted as responsible, while others effectively avoid responsibility, Young (2011) argues for a kind of responsibility that is sensitive to both inequalities and the interconnectedness of current forms of global capitalism. She argues that where someone operates within a system, and gains from that system, they are responsible for the harms that are also generated from that system. Young describes this as the social connection model of responsibility. She specifically draws on the example of sweatshops in low-income earning countries that manufacture products primarily for sale in high-income countries. She suggests that purchasing an item of clothing (a benefit) renders someone politically responsible for the injustices that accrue to those who made it who were subject to awful working conditions (a harm) within a broader global system. There are clear parallels here with climate change, in terms of emitters, and those subject to impacts of climate change. Young also argues for variable levels of responsibility based on the ability and power to respond, act and address such injustices. So here, governments of high-emitting countries and high-emitting corporations bear significant responsibilities. While this variable responsibility was recognised in the first assessment period of the Kyoto Protocol, and subsequently the Paris Agreement, states that are more responsible (emit more and earn more) have systematically sought to evade action. They have not demonstrated this responsibility by actively reducing emissions, preferring offsets or evading actual reductions by buying cheap carbon credits that often don't reflect the emissions reductions they are supposed to (White 2018).

Young's social connection model of responsibility aligns with other social theorists who have raised concerns about the care deficits mentioned above and suggested ways of thinking and acting that address them. Taking responsibility requires care. For example, Puig de la Bellacasa (2012) talks of shifting from an individualistic and atomised way of thinking to one in which caring for others, and relationships with others, both human and non-human as well as those local and further afield is a necessary part of everyday life. Similarly, Tronto (2013) argues that care, even when it is lacking, is fundamental to economic, social and political systems. Unpaid care work as well as paid care work, such as in the hospitality sector, the service sector (including cleaning and rubbish collection) provide the foundations of the more visible, more highly valued economy in society (both in financial and intrinsic terms). By stressing relationships between people, groups and non-humans, as well as the way that care is necessary to everyday political, social and economic life, Tronto argues that care extends beyond the private sphere of one person caring for another, and into the public sphere. It stretches caring from relationships between individuals in private to collective relationships of care (Lawson 2007; also see Bond and Barth 2020). Such a shift has the potential for people to be more explicit about their responsibilities to others because it is underpinned by care and concomitant ethical obligations to avoid or reduce harm. It has the potential to bring out an ethical dimension in responses to climate change that brings justice to the forefront of conversations about responsibility for its impacts.

The activists in our research were clear about the ethical responsibility they felt about engaging in non-violent direct actions, the work in increasing awareness of the causes, interconnections, and the lack of care in government responses to climate change. As reported in Bond, Thomas and Diprose (2020), many participants expressed a strong belief in the 'rightness' of their action, which in turn gave them strength and resilience in the work that they engage in. For example, Rachel argued what they were doing was 'important' and that 'we were pushing at the boundary of something that was very wrong with society and we were there to say "no more"'. Phoebe suggested that the work they were doing in their activism is 'the rent that you pay for living on the planet', and claimed that it wasn't 'a choice' but an 'obligation'. Similarly, Kate said that for her activism invokes 'an ethical obligation to act'.

The participants also noted that this belief in the ethical obligation to act was collective, and they drew strength from this 'collective emotional participation' (Collins 2001, p. 33). Other scholars in social movement theory and studies of activism have explored the value of the emotional connections activists have with one another, and how this sustains their activism, motivation to be engaged, overcome difficulties or unpleasant experiences, and avoid burnout (Bond, Thomas and Diprose 2020; Bosco 2008; Collins 2001; Cox 2009; Juris 2008; Kennelly 2014; Yang 2000). Our participants also noted the value of such collective emotional engagement. In the ANZ Bank action reported on in Chapters 4 and 6, where several activists felt dehumanised by the violent actions of the police and members of the public toward them, they reported that singing, sharing food and connecting with one another afterwards was significant in creating an ethic of care amongst the group. For example, Frankie recalled that they 'were singing and sharing snacks and there was just a really great sense of community'. Similarly, Dennie recalled that afterwards they were 'able to create a space' in which they were 'quite emotionally vulnerable' and 'share these really personal things' about how the action had affected them in different ways. Rachel recalled that these kinds of generative spaces of care were both nurturing and empowering, and that this sustains her activism, giving her strength to keep going. Alongside this interpersonal ethic of care expressed by participants as a result of a particularly challenging action, participants also noted their connection with and care for nature. During a flotilla protest at sea, Moana recalled a moment when several rare toroa (northern royal albatross) landed in the water in a line between the drill ship they were protesting against and the yacht she was aboard. She states, 'it was just really beautiful and [felt like] this really strong message'. Others made similar comments in relation to different actions or everyday activities they were engaged in, from occupying forests to everyday engagements in a veg patch, or walking (see Bond, Thomas and Diprose 2020, pp. 756–757).

The significance of the ethic of care expressed by our participants goes beyond just nurturing their activism. It also speaks to a broader ethic of care that stretches across distance to humans and non-humans that are not in close proximity. This was evident in two ways – distant in time and across geographical distance. First, a small number of our participants were grandparents, and specifically noted the intergenerational justice that they sought through their actions. For example, Dale engaged in non-violent direct action, frequently putting themself in an arrestable position and stated quite emphatically that 'if I can do that for my grandchildren, it makes a difference' (see Bond, Thomas and Diprose 2020, p. 756). Second, the ethic of care expressed by our participants also embraced a sense of responsibility to others well beyond their immediate locality. For example, Sal argues for the need to 'talk more about climate and talk more empathetically about global issues as opposed to just focusing on the local issue' and the desire to create 'a world where we do empathise more with other people [in other countries] and with our environment'. These examples of care for one another within the activist communities, for non-humans and humans in local spaces and also across time (intergenerationally) and space (beyond Aotearoa's shores) is also a source of hope.

The moral imperative that our participants spoke of, and the care ethic that is evident in the activism they engage in reflects the kind of feminist ethic of care that Fisher and Tronto (1990, p. 40) describe, where care is an:

> Activity that includes everything we do to maintain, continue, and repair our 'world' so that we can live in it as well as possible. That world includes our bodies, our selves, and our environment, all of which we seek to interweave in a complex, life-supporting web.

Combining these thoughts on an ethic of care with Young's ideas discussed above, on responsibility for justice as systemic and collective, highlights the point that care invokes responsibility for that thing that is cared for. An additional dimension that Tronto (2013) raises is the idea of 'caring with'. This notion extends directly from caring for or about some thing(s) or some people to a collective culture of care, where care is underpinned by democratic commitments to justice, equity and freedom, in turn enabling an ethical imperative for a collective responsibility to engage in care and justice work. As noted by some of our participants, the very nature of such a collective notion of care and responsibility for justice is subversive. For example, Dan argued that his activism and that of the group was about 'trying to shape the world that we live in, so I guess through that people try to create the communities they wish were normal'. Similarly, Dennie suggested that 'community and friendship are two things capitalism cannot put a price on'. Here they draw on ways of caring with each other, human and non-humans both near and far in time and space to disrupt the kinds of carelessness that is pervasive in the contemporary world and sustain their activism and hope.

Nevertheless, there is also a need to recognise the dark side of care and responsibility, where responsibility and care can inadvertently perpetuate historic structural injustices to which those in privileged positions are often blind. The environmental movement has often been criticised for being very white and middle-class. Although activists are likely passionate and caring about conservation and nature, the relationships with nature experienced by Indigenous peoples and people of colour are not always understood, and are often rendered invisible through the very acts of 'caring' that are engaged in (see, for example, Willems-Braun 1997; Finney 2014; Whyte 2018). Moreover, when care and responsibility extend both through history and beyond the local area or region as is necessary in the context of climate justice, it is 'stretched across space' and time (Raghuram et al. 2009, p. 6). However, in this context there is also a risk that deeply entrenched, often racist, attitudes that exist between the so-called developed world and developing world are perpetuated (Noxolo, Raghuram and Madge 2012). Perhaps rather than care and responsibility for climate justice, this is a kind of 'privileged irresponsibility' (Tronto 2013, p. 64). Indeed, the very framing of a social connection model of justice that Young describes is attuned to structural inequalities and the ways in which they extend through time and space.

In this chapter, we've suggested that contemporary society, particularly in the global North, reflects a generalised lack of care or carelessness. We posed some broad reasons for this, connecting to the separation of the environment from society within Western thought and knowledge systems, and responsibilisation discourses typical in neoliberalism. Drawing on both Iris Marion Young and Joan Tronto's framings of responsibility and care, and how these were expressed by the activists in our study, we showed the possibilities that such a 'caring democracy' (Tronto 2013) has for subverting these entrenched ways of thinking and being in the world. Such subversions show the importance of the ongoing labour that activists seeking climate justice engage in to carve open democratic spaces that create the possibilities for alternative future imaginaries that are more hopeful.

8

Democracy and Hope

A DEMOCRATIC ETHOS FOR CHANGE

In this final brief chapter, we reflect on the work of the activists who participated in our research in Aotearoa New Zealand within the context of global narratives of climate change and the necessity of a kind of environmental democracy that keeps on pushing for justice and change. In our view, democracy requires open robust debate on ideas and values, opening possibilities and pushing at the boundaries of what is 'conventional wisdom' at any one time. This is not an unfettered free speech though – liberal freedoms need to be paired with democratic responsibilities and an ethic of care and respect. We reject any claims, made through the guise of free speech, that denies the existence of particular people. Democratic responsibilities, care and respect necessitate a clear-eyed assessment of the causes of climate change, specifically racial capitalism that extracts value from people, specifically Indigenous folks and people of colour, and nature. Racial capitalism has made it possible for 10 per cent of the global population to be responsible for 52 per cent of cumulative carbon emissions (Oxfam 2020), where corporate sponsorship is used to offset the huge bill for policing COPs against climate justice activists (Ambrose 2021), and where the fossil fuel industry had the largest delegation at COP26 (McGrath 2021).

It is only through a vibrant democracy that meaningful change can occur. However 'conventional wisdom' is presented in society in ways that are constantly reinterpreted and re-presented and this has significant effects that are complicated. As we've shown, these processes of contesting socially and environmentally destructive 'conventional wisdoms' are entangled in government institutions and agencies, legislative regimes, media reporting, social media and the social norms in society. Some of these are historical legacies (like the violence of colonialism) that continue to be deeply (re)embedded in the present. The impacts of climate change and the consequences of inadequate action to mitigate these impacts are imagined in vastly different ways.

Some of the tensions between the ways both the causes and the consequences of climate change are imagined can undermine the work that activists have already undertaken to create change. For example, there are many working on emission mitigation measures who believe the current system simply needs reforming, while others in the climate justice movement argue that the only way to address climate change is through overthrowing the racial capitalist system. Similarly, in terms of the consequences of climate change, there is the very real anxiety that the change that has occurred is not enough or is not happening fast enough. For some, that will push them to fight harder for the change they see is needed. For others, it will be paralysing. There is a fine line between narratives that provide for hope to imagine a climate-altered future that is just and makes the world liveable, and those that compound eco-anxiety, despair and hopelessness. We are struck by the energy, passion and labour that has gone into creating spaces for debate and dissent in relation to climate change both here in Aotearoa New Zealand and abroad. And there have been significant wins. But at the same time, we feel frustration at the persistent efforts to maintain business-as-usual and to subvert the reality as we see it with fake news, downplayed risks, and political and economic protectionism. In this chapter, we pick up these tensions and contradictions to attempt to wind a pathway through them, to acknowledge and celebrate the work done, but recognise the mountain still to climb without resorting to despair and apocalyptic imaginaries.

TENSIONS IN DIVERSITY

At the time of writing, following the IPCC's release of the sixth assessment report, the *Guardian* newspaper published an article entitled '"Code red for Humanity": what the papers say about the IPCC report on the climate crisis' with a collage of headlines from across UK print media. Terms reflected the full array of narratives we have seen while we've been engaged in the research reported in this book, from muted responses calling for more green technological fixes to calls for an 'urgent road map' to deal with the climate crisis, to headlines including the words 'code red', 'irreversible', 'crisis', and others describing the IPCC's report as a 'doomsday report on apocalyptic climate change' (Sullivan 2021). The article reviews the full range of the kinds of responses to climate change that we have become familiar with in our study, from a blue-green techno-fix (as we'd call it in Aotearoa where blue represents the centre-right perspective), to the call for urgent action to the climate crisis, to apocalyptic doomsayers. Each also reflects a response that shifts from creating change within business-as-usual through to demands for revolution or system change.

This spectrum of positions is often also reflected in different groups from within the broader climate justice movement – those that engage in non-violent direct action like Extinction Rebellion, through to those who are actively lobbying politicians and see their role specifically as working within the system to generate change through increased regulation and policy shifts. There is sometimes tension between these different groups. This has been evident to Sophie over the last six years in teaching a course on Geographies of Contestation, which involved a symposium in which local groups present their social action work on a range of issues to the students. Most years, the symposium included two climate change groups – one national-level group that represented young people who were actively engaged within the political system and were instrumental in pushing the government toward enacting what has been dubbed as the Zero Carbon Act (enacted in 2019). The other was a local Oil Free group who engaged in non-violent direct action. In subsequent discussions with students in the early years, they frequently commented on the evident tensions between the groups, suggesting they were needless, and that they should work more in solidarity (in the last few years they have been). The students also reflected on the different ways climate change was framed and its implications for humans. Some preferred a hopeful framing, others specifically draw on apocalyptic narratives to urge action.

These tensions are also clear in the ways in which some more 'radical' forms of activism sometimes dismiss those that are seen as institutionalised (Berny and Rootes 2018). This is most evident in critiques of large ENGOs, like Greenpeace, who are accused of complicity when they become corporatised, even while maintaining campaigns engaging in more radical forms of non-violent direct action. But large ENGOs like 350 Aotearoa (350.org's Aotearoa branch) and Greenpeace Aotearoa, play a crucial role in coordinating some climate movement actions, and often in resourcing or supporting actions like the ANZ blockades reported on in previous chapters. This is especially so in terms of co-ordinating actions at sea requiring ocean-going yachts and sailing expertise and in providing legal support for protestors. In some cases, legal representation offered by an ENGO on a pro bono basis makes the difference between whether or not an activist will engage in an action that puts them in an arrestable position. This pattern of support by large ENGOs for smaller, perhaps anarchist climate groups has been noted in other industrialised countries, highlighting more synergistic relationships (see Berny and Rootes 2018). Nevertheless, tensions can occur in local actions between large ENGOs and smaller local groups when decisions are made as to who or what actions are supported, or when there are disagreements as to how an action should be undertaken, which can be divisive and can reflect the tension between radicalism and reformism, or radicals and moderates (Haines 1984).

We suggest that as part of a commitment to a vibrant environmental democracy, there is value in acknowledging the full range of actions within this spectrum between radicalism and more moderate actions, and this also involves acknowledging the full range of narratives that emerge along with them. As Scobie, Milne and Love (2020) note, Māori struggles for rangatiratanga and environmental movements have often involved struggle within 'common sense' institutions while also struggling against and outside them at the same time. However, this is also fraught in three ways. First, it is challenging in the face of the power of those who continually seek to maintain business-as-usual and who work to close down these spaces of debate, as documented in previous chapters. Second, the diversity of narratives that emerge trouble and expose already existing structural injustices – the racism, sexism and classism that exists across society is also very much present amongst actors seeking to address climate change. While the very definition of the climate justice movement acknowledges these power dynamics and seeks to address them, they remain deeply entrenched in the subjectivities of many activists. Third, there is also a need to simultaneously keep a keen eye on the effects different narratives have on how people, communities and nation-states respond to the threats of a changing climate and their own eco-anxiety. Paralysis will not address climate change or the structural injustices that are part of the climate changing capitalist system. These challenges are significant and strengthen an argument for increasing open democratic debate that is underpinned by an awareness of the way racial capitalism underpins the climate crisis.

GLOBAL NARRATIVES OF CLIMATE CHANGE

Since beginning this research, we have been aware of the way in which climate change narratives have shifted, and the movement has gained momentum (Rosewarne, Goodman and Pearse 2013). The extent of climate denialism, while still disturbingly present, appears to have reduced, and mainstream global newspapers (admittedly, those more commonly associated with the left of the political spectrum) frequently report on the 'climate crisis' (e.g. *The Guardian*), or have explicitly expressed a commitment to report new scientific evidence (e.g. Stuff.co.nz in Aotearoa New Zealand, an online mainstream news platform). This is further reflected in the proliferation of a range of activist groups with global reach and impact. At the time of writing, Extinction Rebellion's global website claims there are over 1,100 XR groups in 82 countries. Similarly, 350.org has branches all over the globe and has also initiated a number of global actions and campaigns since the International Day of Climate Action in 2009, with numbers and uptake increasing over time. These include the People's Climate March in 2014, the fossil fuel divestment campaigns, such as the one discussed in Chapter 4, and the 2019 Global Climate Strike. The latter was, of course, the initiative that followed from Greta Thunberg's School Strike 4 Climate or Fridays for Future movement.

The impact of the School Strike 4 Climate is significant, in that it shifted concern for climate change into protest action by many who would not otherwise have participated. It highlighted the intergenerational injustices of climate change in a new and pressing way. Australia and Aotearoa New Zealand followed a slightly different trajectory than elsewhere. Many countries, including the UK, adopted 'Fridays for Future', in which tens of thousands of students engaged in weekly school strikes (McKnight 2020). In Australia and Aotearoa, less regular but larger strikes occurred, taking the name School Strike 4 Climate (Handford and Maeder 2020). Initially, there was much debate in the media about whether young people should be 'skipping school' and that instead they should be learning for the future, that children were not really concerned about the climate but were just opportunistically taking a day off, or that they should 'strike' at the weekend (Bray 2020; Handford and Maeder 2020; Thomas, Cretney and Hayward 2019). However, the time of the Global Climate Strike in September 2019, which was run in conjunction with 350.org and involving not just young people but all those who stood with them, demonstrated a much higher level of mainstream public engagement. The explicit and moral argument within the Fridays for Future and School Strike 4 Climate is based on intergenerational justice, and demands that current generations, particularly those in power, assume responsibility for the harms that current and past generations have and are causing future generations. The global narrative is relatively positively framed, rights-based and underpinned by a moral sensibility. The demands for climate justice were striking in the context of our research. When we began this project, climate justice was very much a fringe concept. In September 2019, the concept framed the whole strike, an event involving 3.5 per cent of Aotearoa New Zealand's total population (*RNZ* 2019).

In contrast, the narratives of groups like Extinction Rebellion are oriented toward raising awareness of the significant impacts of a climate altered future, should business-as-usual continue. Their campaign to 'tell the truth' involves reporting on a range of scientific documents to draw out evidence on climate change science and impacts, document various governments' (in)action around the world, and pick up on claims that the earth is entering its sixth phase of mass extinctions (see https://rebellion.global/blog/2020/12/11/tell-the-truth/). From this they claim to be a movement that seeks change that avoids human extinction and ecological collapse. XR's distinct repertoire of tactics and strategies includes various radical forms of non-violent direct action, often explicitly placing activists in situations that provoke the police to arrest them. This has been the subject of significant critique, particularly in the UK where the tactic demonstrates the white middle-class privilege of the majority of members (Adams 2019; Charles 2019; Saunders, Doherty and Hayes 2020; Wretched of the Earth 2019; Zapata 2020 – discussed further below). Nevertheless, these tactics have in a very short time, engaged significant numbers of protestors in the UK and elsewhere.

Both XR and the youth-led climate strikes build on a longer trajectory of activism by Indigenous people, peasants (as self-identified in movements like La Via Campesina), and folks from small island states. In 2014, acutely aware of narratives rendering Pacific peoples as 'vulnerable', small and needy (see Hau'ofa 1994), the Pacific Climate Warriors blockaded the Newcastle Coal Port in Newcastle, Australia, the largest of its type in the world. Activists representing twelve Pacific nations, supported by hundreds of Australians, stopped ten coal ships passing through the port and asserted they were not drowning, they were fighting (Packard 2014). In a speech to COP26, India Logan-Riley, a young Māori climate activist, located the roots of climate change in hundreds of years of imperialism, and argued that Indigenous resistance to capitalist extraction had prevented huge amounts of greenhouse gas emissions (*RNZ* 2021b).

We suggest that the success and strength of these global narratives demanding action on climate change lies in their diversity, dynamism and persistence. There may be tensions between different groups about the nature of action that is thought best to achieve change and the nature of that change. However, the range of differences between groups means they appeal to a wider range of audiences, generating possibilities for enrolling a wider demographic and so increasing pressure on governments and corporations for action. Moreover, the radical flank effect of more 'edgy' activism, such as those engaging in civil disobedience, non-violent direct action, and attention grabbing spectacular and often illegal actions, opens a space in which more moderate forms of action becomes more accessible to a wider audience. Despite the potentially paralysing narratives of emergency, urgency, doom and apocalypse, recognising the diversity of forms of global climate action ensures that it is still valued for the change so far achieved.

Nevertheless, there is a need to recognise the power dynamics within these campaigns. As the Wretched of the Earth stated in their open letter to XR in the UK:

> the bleakness is not something of 'the future'. For those of us who are indigenous, working class, black, brown, queer, trans or disabled, the experience of structural violence became part of our birthright. Greta Thunberg calls world leaders to act by reminding them that 'Our house is on fire'. For many of us, the house has been on fire for a long time: whenever the tide of ecological violence rises, our communities, especially in the Global South are always first hit. We are the first to face poor air quality, hunger, public health crises, drought, floods and displacement. (Wretched of the Earth 2019)

Similarly, Geoff Mann, writing on 'Doom', and the nature of apocalyptic narratives that are invoked in relation to climate change and other contemporary global crises recognises the erasure of the past (and present) that such narratives evoke. He writes,

> just as colonialism is not a past event, but an ongoing process, doom is not confined to the future, but have a long history among the planet's poorest and most exploited peoples, both within and beyond the societies that call themselves 'modern'. (Mann 2019, p. 102)

Recognition of the unevenness and invisibilities within climate action and the apocalyptic narratives of the climate emergency highlights the justice dimension of climate justice. Mann suggests that such 'doom' narratives have a place, but need to acknowledge what has gone before, while assuming collective responsibility for the present and confronting the reality of change. 'One does not need to share this sense of doom to be forced to take it seriously' (Mann 2019, p. 102; see also Cretney and Nissen 2019). In thinking through these dynamics, the unevenness and instances of white control of the climate justice movement, its wins but also the work still to be done, we tread a fine line between being hopeful and real in terms of the successes of the climate justice movement in Aotearoa New Zealand.

SHIFTING NARRATIVES IN AOTEAROA NEW ZEALAND

In 2018, following an election campaign in the previous year in which Jacinda Ardern stated that climate change was her generation's 'nuclear free moment', the new coalition government in Aotearoa New Zealand banned any new oil and gas exploration in the Exclusive Economic Zone. Existing permits were unaffected by the ban, and an exception was made for onshore production in Taranaki, a region on the west coast of the country where all commercial production is centred. By the beginning of 2021, all remaining offshore exploration permits had been relinquished, with companies claiming a combination of the pandemic and pricing uncertainties as the primary reasons for withdrawal. Handford and Maeder (2020, p. 221) state that 'this was a monumental win for the Aotearoa New Zealand climate movement and a testament to the power of grassroots, people-powered movements'. Others within the Oil Free movement have similarly claimed the success as theirs (Allott 2021; Oil Free Otago 2021; Young 2021). Yet such a 'win' could be precarious, with the opposition party claiming that they will repeal the legislation that provides for the ban on new oil and gas exploration if they are re-elected (1 News 2020). Handford and Maeder (2020) also acknowledge that despite the 'win', there are clear indications that fossil fuel extraction and production is far from over, given the exception area in Taranaki, and noting that even while announcing the ban in 2018 the government:

> opened up 2200 square kilometres of land for potential oil and gas drilling, a move that was heavily criticized by School Strikers, environ-

mental groups and local Iwi. This shows that fossil fuel development is far from over in Aotearoa. (p. 221)

Moreover, Aotearoa New Zealand is the third highest (behind USA and Australia) per capita emitter of greenhouse gases (GHGs) amongst Annex 1 countries in the UNFCCC (Ministry for the Environment 2021). The government response to climate change has been poor and recent initiatives are underwhelming. So there is still much to do. Despite the narratives of care that have emerged under Prime Minister Ardern's leadership, including in relation to a successful early response to the global pandemic, Aotearoa New Zealand remains one of the most neoliberalised countries in the OECD, and has some extreme inequalities, affecting Māori and Pasifika disproportionately. Previous research in geography and on environmental justice has commented on the 'whiteness' of the environmental movement within Western contexts for decades (Bond, Diprose and McGregor 2015; Pulido 2015; Taylor 2002, 2014; Willems-Braun 1997). This whiteness was exposed in Aotearoa New Zealand's climate movement recently in three (inter-related) ways forcing some in the movement to reflect on their complicity within this racism.

First, on 15 March 2019, while thousands of students across Aotearoa New Zealand went on strike demanding action on climate change, many Pasifika students engaged in the first day of Polyfest.[1] Polyfest is a national celebration, and as suggested by Lourdes Vano, a young Cook Island, Samoan New Zealander, 'one of the biggest expressions of our culture available to us here in Aotearoa' (Vano 2019). The clash of events was stark – students from some of the communities most affected by and least responsible for climate change were forced to choose between a day dedicated to cultural celebration, and striking for climate justice. It was also the same day that a terrorist, and self-declared eco-fascist, shot and killed 51 people at two central city mosques in Ōtautahi Christchurch, injuring and traumatising dozens of others. As Thomas, Cretney and Hayward (2019) note, 'the intersection of the events – the strikes and the massacre – highlight the need to democratise responses to climate change' (p. 98). They go on to note that it's clear through the placards and messaging used in School Strike 4 Climate that it is oriented toward climate justice and care. Yet it still doesn't go far enough in acknowledging the extent to which climate change and the movement's responses to it are still embedded within contemporary colonialism and associated racisms.

The second, and related, series of events demonstrate a shift in some parts of the climate movement. As a result of scheduling the School Strike to clash with Polyfest, a young Samoan New Zealander, Aigagalefili Fepulea'i Tapua'i with others established a group 4 Tha Kulture, to represent 'brown voices' and 'Southside', referring to South Auckland which has a high proportion of Pasifika people living and working there (Lee 2019). In their work, they have sought to highlight both the racism that is inherent in the lack of a voice given to Pasifika people, as well as educating and raising awareness of the impacts of climate change and what it means for Pasifika people.

These kinds of exclusions are made throughout society in everyday ways, demonstrating the entrenched discrimination that is at their foundation. For example, in response to the release of the most recent IPCC Report, Radio New Zealand, a centrist national radio service, hosted a panel interview with three different climate action groups (*RNZ* 2021a). The groups were the Pacific Climate Warriors (the Auckland branch of the International Pacific Climate Warriors who operate as part of 350Pacific); Te Ara Whatu (an Indigenous climate justice group, who formed in 2017 when they sent the country's first Indigenous youth delegation to the UN Climate talks); and Generation Zero (established over ten years ago and now have a relatively high profile in Aotearoa through lobbying government on a range of policy initiatives). The latter group are predominantly pākehā (white). What was notable in this interview was that the pākehā group representative (a male) was invited to speak first, commenting directly on the technical information in the IPCC Report. The two Indigenous groups (both represented by women) initially had questions addressed to them asking specifically about the Indigenous groups they represent, rather than climate change impacts directly. At one point, the woman from Te Ara Whatu stated that there was a role for Indigenous knowledge and wisdom – mātauranga in te reo – and that Indigenous people did not create the conditions that have caused climate change, but Indigenous groups hold solutions. The interviewer responded with a follow up question that asked about these 'ways of helping' (*RNZ* 2021a), immediately privileging Western science over the potential 'help' that mātauranga can provide. The woman from Te Ara Whatu went on to say:

> Even though we might be given a space at the table, whatever our mātauranga is, it isn't gonna work under the construct of *your* system

and *your* table so in order for our voices to be heard we need people to create systems and structures where our voices can be heard. (Jakicevich in *RNZ* 2021a, emphasis in original audio)

Tellingly, the interviewer did not respond directly to this, and instead provided the final word on the question of hope to the male pākehā representative of Generation Zero.

While we have no intention of undermining the important work Generation Zero have done over the last decade or so, the interview and the privilege given to the pākehā male participant demonstrates two highly problematic characteristics of the climate movement. On one hand, it highlights how Western science is elevated over mātauranga or Indigenous knowledge. Specifically in relation to climate change, Indigenous knowledge is typically valued as a 'supplement' to Western knowledge in the context of climate change, rather than as valuable solutions in its own right (Whyte 2017b). On the other hand, it highlights the way Māori and Pasifika groups are invisibilised within the movement. Indigenous groups such as Te Ara Whatu, the Pacific Climate Warriors and 4 Tha Kulture have been demanding action on climate change for some time, some for a decade or more. This was noted in a recent news article, that cited 'wavemaker' (Indigenous concept of an activist), Luhama Taualupe, who observed how when white European Greta Thunberg engaged in climate action, people took notice even though Pasifika people have engaged in climate action for decades. She was quoted as saying:

People are only willing to genuinely listen when somebody they feel comfortable listening to is talking to them and doesn't seem like a threat. That's a difficult thing because that's subconscious racial bias. (Cited in Cardwell 2021)

The third event that demonstrates a degree of shift in the climate movement in Aotearoa New Zealand is the disbandment of the Auckland branch of School Strike 4 Climate in response to the growing recognition of their own complicity in these ongoing everyday colonialisms (Cretney and Nissen 2019). The Auckland group formally apologised, stating that this was overdue, and that:

We apologise for the hurt, burnout, and trauma. We also apologise for the further trauma caused by our slow action to take responsibility. We recognise that this apology can never be enough to make up for our actions on top of years of systemic and systematic oppression, racism, and the silencing of those who are the most affected by climate change. This apology is just one of our steps in taking accountability for our actions. (Cited in Cardwell 2021)

The reception to this was mixed. For some Māori and Pacific activists, this recognition and stepping aside was overdue. White voices, white ideas had dominated climate activism for too long. For others, it seemed like a familiar dynamic whereby white communities fail to do the work of fixing the damage done by Eurocentricism and capitalism.

Underpinning these debates is Te Tiriti o Waitangi. We discussed at the start of the book the founding document of this country, a treaty that Māori signed to protect ongoing Māori sovereignty. As we noted, Māori and some pākehā continue to demand that Te Tiriti is upheld. We have also argued that addressing climate change requires confronting systems of injustice rather than individual behaviour change or market solutions. Ongoing colonialism is one of the systems that needs to be confronted within our societies, and within activist groups. More and more activist groups in Aotearoa New Zealand are grappling with how to do this within their own organising, the actions they take and the visions for the future they propose. There is a lot of work to do, and figuring out how to balance Māori leadership with non-Indigenous commitments to doing the labour is not always easy.

This is a journey we as a research team are on too. All three of us are pākehā, and we have uncertainly navigated how to do this research in a way that begins from Te Tiriti and an acknowledgment of unceded Māori sovereignty. We built good relationships with many activist groups but were less successful with many of the hapū and iwi leading climate justice and Oil Free struggles. We were hampered by our shallow networks and awkwardness about how to build good, trusting relationships. While we have built some enduring relationships, almost ten years since we first started this inquiry, we think about how we would do things differently so that this research more successfully engaged with decolonisation and ethics of restoration and interdependence (Elkington et al. 2020). As we continue this work, we offer some final thoughts reflecting on our research and ongoing observations of the climate justice movement in Aotearoa New Zealand.

PUSHING THE BOUNDARIES OF WHAT IS POSSIBLE

Looking back on the Oil Free campaign, it is clear there have been significant shifts. In Chapter 4, we documented how the campaign drew on eco-nationalist discourses with the moniker 'no drill, no spill', drawing on specific values around access to beaches, and fear of pollution. Research participants explicitly stated at the time, that although they were climate justice advocates and were campaigning for action on climate change, this was an approach that they felt would get more people on board. At the time in about 2014, they were clear that discussing climate change was not palatable, and would turn people off, relegating their work to the fringes. Thankfully, that is no longer the case, given the increasing public discussion on climate change as noted above. When we began our research, the media was mixed in its reporting on the urgency of climate change, treating proponents of the climate movement with disdain, always raising the question of the economy, jobs and employment associated with big oil and gas as a counter to any demands for action on climate change. Now, it seems the pendulum has shifted a little, and the media profiles big emitters with disdain, and in some cases has explicitly committed to reporting the science of climate change accurately (as indicated above). However, these shifts are tempered by increasing surveillance, uneven policing practices, and ongoing colonialism and racism. As Pulido (2015) argues, these structural injustices are an inherent part of the economic system of capitalism which is and always has been founded on racial and class-based hierarchies. The discussion above highlights the challenges of the fine line we tread. While there is some momentum toward change and celebrating wins is important in maintaining hope, there is a need to recognise the work still to do. And this is challenging work. In navigating this path, we suggest two things: an ethical platform and imagination.

First, the ethical platform is a principle of robust environmental democracy. Although 'democracy' in its various practised forms does not reflect this principle, and democracy has been a tool for colonialism and privilege, our vision of democracy is quite different. It is aspirational, and recognises the value of all voices, of open, honest, respectful debate, and is underpinned by ethical values of care and responsibility (Bond 2019). We have already indicated above that the environmental democracy we envisage does not condone unfettered free speech. This seems crucial in the world of fake news, social media, suspicion of science and authority, and conspiracy theories. There is no easy solution to this until governments and the corporate owners of social media and similar platforms take responsibility for the injustices that hate speech and other forms of violence and oppression that online platforms enable. Moreover, we argue that while 'listening to the science' as advocated by many in the climate justice movement is important, there is a desperate need for an ethical basis on which to act (Evensen 2019). We have already suggested that neoliberal capitalism provides numerous ways to ignore emotion, care and harm to humans and non-humans which further justifies the urgency with which such an ethical foundation needs to be embedded in Western society in particular.

In practice, a democratic ethos looks like collective care for humans and non-humans and the planet. More than that, there is care for other ontologies and worlds. It takes an expansive view of time; while it looks to the future to imagine more just sustainable ways of being, it also draws on the past, and who and what was sacrificed, while engaging in practices located in the present (Parsons, Fisher and Crease 2021). A democratic ethos is attuned to structural injustice, and identifies and critiques systems that perpetuate privilege. Addressing these injustices is a shared and collective endeavour, and solutions are reached through robust discussion that is underpinned by respect and openness. From the context of Aotearoa New Zealand, recent work on constitutional transformation led initially by Moana Jackson and Margaret Mutu reflects a democratic ethos, where new possibilities for a Te Tiriti-based constitution were developed through many kōrero (conversations) with Māori across the country. The report, entitled *Matike Mai* (2016), provides examples of alternative constitutional arrangements that embraces a rangatiratanga sphere and a sphere of the Crown or a kāwanatanga sphere, and a relational sphere in between. A second related example lies in the work of Maria Bargh (2019) who has written about a 'tika transition', a shift of society and economy that is in conversation with international law, but upholds what is tika, or right and just, within a Māori context. A tika transition upholds Te Tiriti, bolsters and respects rangatiratanga, Māori authority. Many initiatives in a tika transition take shape in the relational sphere, between kāwanatanga and rangatiratanga, as the transformative action needed is negotiated (Bargh and Tapsell 2021; *Matike Mai* 2016). Bargh and Tapsell (2021, p. 20) argue that:

> Increasing recognition of tikanga and te ao Māori by the Crown and non-Māori has provided reaffirmation for hapū and iwi Māori who

have continued to practice tikanga in diverse and changing ways, and it provides hope that modest and bolder steps in a tika direction might continue to proliferate.

Many Indigenous peoples' cultures and scholarship have such ethical foundations at their core. And despite the erosion of ethics in Western thought and culture, there are thinkers (particularly feminist scholars) who continue to advocate for an ethic of care (as discussed in Chapter 7). We suggest Young's (2011) responsibility for justice provides space for recognition of the long histories of marginalisation and disadvantage that many people have experienced, and for whom climate change is just a continuation of past processes of oppression and violence. Tronto's (2013) 'caring democracy' through which the erosion of care evident under neoliberal capitalism is addressed, provides space for centring care for human and non-human nature. We argue that such an 'ethos of democracy' has the potential to shift debates away from how much climate change mitigation or adaptation costs, to focusing on human and non-human wellbeing and flourishing, enabling all people to live well in ways that are determined by communities and groups, not by those in privileged positions of power.

Second, we argue for the importance of imagination. Elsewhere, Amanda has written of imagination as a spectrum of possibilities:

At one end, it builds on what we know and is conceivable within our existing worlds. ... At the other end of the spectrum, imagination remakes things entirely and goes beyond what we currently know. This involves interrogating the existing categories that constrain where our imagination might go, and attempting to transgress them. This is the kind of imagination where social relations are entirely remade and the world is fantastically different. Across this spectrum, the act of imagining utopias has radical potential... (Thomas 2019, pp. 164–165)

Hope sits somewhere within that spectrum, enabling possible futures to be thought and alleviating the kind of eco-anxiety that permeates everyday life (Cretney and Nissen 2019; Thomas, Cretney and Hayward 2019). The example of the Oil Free campaign in Aotearoa New Zealand shows the constant struggle between imagining and actioning change and imagining impossible futures within the constellation of narratives about a global apocalypse. Imagination is a means to envision what might seem to be impossible and to make it possible and real. It provides goals to strive toward, and enables hope that motivates and energises. Through a robust environmental democracy, alternative futures can be imagined and fought for. So while there is more hard work to do, specifically in relation to shifting entrenched structural injustices and decolonising activist groups, we are energised by the work already being done. With hope, imagination and voice, alternative futures are always possible.

Notes

CHAPTER 1

1. Te Tiriti o Waitangi and The Treaty of Waitangi are different documents with different meanings central to the constitutional foundations of contemporary Aotearoa New Zealand. The former is in te reo Māori, the Māori language, and was the text signed by most chiefs. It is also the text that holds sway in international law. The latter is an English language text that, unlike Te Tiriti, passes sovereignty from Māori to the British Crown. After decades and decades of Māori activism, there is growing recognition of Te Tiriti. In this book, we talk about both texts, and the blurry space where it is unclear which is being invoked. The differences and the implications of these differences are discussed in more detail in the next chapter.

CHAPTER 2

1. For further information, see Te Arawhiti – the Office of Māori-Crown Relations quarterly reports at www.govt.nz/assets/Documents/OTS/Quarterly-reports/Quarterly-report-to-31-March-2021.pdf.
2. Kaitiakitanga refers to the guardianship and care that Māori have toward their territory, territory that they are genealogically connected to.
3. All the submissions and advice related to the Bill's passage through Parliament is available here: https://www.parliament.nz/en/pb/bills-and-laws/bills-proposed-laws/document/00DBHOH_BILL11023_1/exclusive-economic-zone-and-continental-shelf-environmental

CHAPTER 4

1. ANZ disputed the investment numbers claimed by activists.

CHAPTER 5

1. The code of conduct says that state services must be fair, impartial, responsible and trustworthy. More detail can be found here: www.publicservice.govt.nz/assets/Legacy/resources/Code-of-conduct-StateServices.pdf.

CHAPTER 8

1. A number of Pacific ethnic groups live in Aotearoa New Zealand, often described as Pasifika (although this term is contested). Pasifika peoples comprise some 7.4 per cent of the population and of these, almost two-thirds are born in Aotearoa New Zealand. Pasifika nations have long and complex colonial relationships with Aotearoa New Zealand (Pasefika Proud 2016).

References

1 News, 'Todd Muller Commits to National's Pledge to Raise Superannuation Age, Bring Back Oil and Gas Exploration', *1 News*, 25 May 2020. www.1news.co. nz/2020/05/25/todd-muller-commits-to-nationals-pledge-to-raise-superannuation-age-bring-back-oil-and-gas-exploration/ (accessed 6 December 2021).

3 News, 'Greenpeace Blocks Entrance to Statoil in Wellington', *Three News*, 2014. www.3news.co.nz/nznews/greenpeace-blocks-entrance-to-statoilin-wellington-2014121008#axzz3ZVkYCVdo (accessed 15 September 2014).

Adams, N., 'Let's Talk about Extinction Rebellion', *Thinking Doing Changing*, 18 April 2019, https://thinkingdoingchanging.com/2019/04/18/lets-talk-about-extinction-rebellion/ (accessed 5 December 2021).

Aikman, P.J.W.E., 'Trouble on the Frontier: Hunt for the Wilderpeople, Sovereignty and State Violence', *SITES: New Series* 14/1 (2017): 56–79. https://search.informit.org/doi/10.3316/informit.960863505602793.

Allen, J.M. and Bruce, T., 'Constructing the Other. News Media Representations of a Predominantly "Brown" Community in New Zealand', *Pacific Journalism Review: Te Koakoa* 23/1 (2017): 225–244. https://doi.org/10.24135/pjr.v23i1.33.

Allott, A., 'Last South Island Deep Sea Oil Exploration Permit Dropped', *Stuff*, 10 March 2021, www.stuff.co.nz/environment/climate-news/124496214/last-south-island-deepsea-oil-exploration-permit-dropped (accessed 5 December 2021).

Ambrose, J., 'Cop26 Corporate Sponsors Condemn Climate Summit as "Mismanaged"', *The Guardian*, 17 October 2021, www.theguardian.com/environment/2021/oct/17/cop26-corporate-sponsors-condemn-climate-summit-as-mismanaged (accessed 3 December 2021).

Anae, M. *The Platform: The Radical Legacy of the Polynesian Panthers* (Bridget Williams Books, 2020).

Anae, M., Iuli, L. and Tamu, L. *Polynesian Panthers: Pacific Protest and Affirmative Action in Aotearoa New Zealand 1971–1981* (Huia Publishers, 2015).

Askins, K. and Swanson, K. 'Holding onto Emotions: A Call to Action in Academia', *Emotion, Space and Society* 33 (2019): 100617. https://doi.org/10.1016/j.emospa.2019.100617.

Australian Associated Press, 'Victoria Police Defend Actions at Imarc Mining Protest after Activist Hospitalised', *The Guardian*, 30 October 2019, www.theguardian.com/australia-news/2019/oct/30/melbourne-police-arrest-12-on-second-day-of-climate-protest-at-imarc-mining-conference (accessed 10 August 2021).

Baker, T. and Davis, C. 'Everyday Resistance to Workfare: Welfare Beneficiary Advocacy in Auckland, New Zealand', *Social Policy and Society* 17/4 (2018): 535–546. https://doi.org/10.1017/S1474746417000306.

Banks, G.A., Scheyvens, R.A., McLennan, S.J. and Bebbington, A. 'Conceptualising Corporate Community Development', *Third World Quarterly* 37/2 (2016): 245–263. https://doi.org/10.1080/01436597.2015.1111135.

Bargh, M. (ed.), *Resistance: An Indigenous Response to Neoliberalism* (Huia Publishers, 2007).

Bargh, M. 'Community Organizing: Māori Movement-building', in A. Choudry, J. Hanley and E. Shragge (eds), *Organize! Building from the Local for Global Justice* (PM Press, 2012), pp. 123–131.

Bargh, M., 'A Tika Transition', in D. Hall (ed.), *A Careful Revolution: Towards a Low-emissions Future* (Bridget Williams Books, 2019).

Bargh, M. and Tapsell, E., 'For a Tika Transition Strengthen Rangatiratanga', *Policy Quarterly* 17/3 (2021): 13–22.

Baxter, J., Kingi, T., Tapsell, R. and Durie, M. 'Māori', in M. Oakley-Browne, E. Wells and K. Scott (eds), *Te rau hinengaro: The New Zealand Mental Health Survey* (New Zealand Ministry of Health, 2006).

Bawaka Country, Suchet-Pearson, S., Wright, S., Lloyd, K., Tofa, M., Sweeney, J., Burarrwanga, L., Ganambarr, R., Ganambarr-Stubbs, M., Ganambarr, B. and Maymuru, D., 2019. 'Goŋ Gurtha: Enacting Response-Abilities as Situated Co-becoming', *Environment and Planning D: Society and Space* 37/4 (2019): 682–702. https://doi.org/10.1177%2F0263775818799749.

Bell, C., *Inventing New Zealand: Everyday Myths of Pakeha Identity* (Penguin Press, 1996).

Benford, R.D. and Snow, D.A., 'Framing Processes and Social Movements: An Overview and Assessment', *Annual Review of Sociology* 26/1 (2000): 611–639. www.jstor.org/stable/223459.

Bennett, A., 'Poll Backing for More Mineral Searches Cheers Key', *New Zealand Herald*, 5 July 2012, www.nzherald.co.nz/business/poll-backing-for-more-mineral-searches-cheers-key/DLY3JEN4L6NMHMWXOCFIJKTRRY/ (accessed 26 November 2021).

Berny, N. and Rootes, C., 'Environmental NGOs at a Crossroads?', *Environmental Politics* 27/6 (2018): 947–972. https://doi.org/10.1080/09644016.2018.153629 3.

Bingham, E. and Penfold, P., 'Thompson and Clark Hosted Oil Industry Meeting in "bunker" Underneath Beehive', *Stuff*, 18 September 2018, www.stuff.co.nz/national/stuff-circuit/107136659/thompson--clark-hosted-oil-industry-meeting-in-bunker-underneath-beehive (accessed 26 November 2021).

Bond, S., 'A Democratic Ethos', *Keywords in Radical Geography: Antipode at 50* (2019): 14–19. https://onlinelibrary.wiley.com/doi/pdf/10.1002/9781119 558071.

Bond, S. and Barth, J. 'Care-full and Just: Making a Difference through Climate Change Adaptation', *Cities* 102 (2020): 102734. https://doi.org/10.1016/j.cities.2020.102734.

Bond, S., Diprose, G. and McGregor, A. '2 Precious 2 Mine: Post Politics, Colonial Imaginary or Hopeful Political Moment?', *Antipode* 47 (2015): 1161–1183. https://doi.org/10.1111/anti.12157.

Bond, S., Diprose, G. and Thomas, A.C., 'Contesting Deep Sea Oil: Politicisation–Depoliticisation–Repoliticisation', *Environment and Planning C: Politics and Space* 37/3 (2019): 519–538. https://doi.org/10.1177/2399654418788675.

Bond, S., Thomas, A. and Diprose, G., 'Making and Unmaking Political Subjectivities: Climate Justice, Activism, and Care', *Transactions of the Institute of British Geographers* 45/4, (2020): 750–762. https://doi.org/10.1111/tran.12382.

Bosco, F.J. 'Emotions that Build Networks: Geographies of Human Rights Movements in Argentina and Beyond', *Tijdschrift voor Economis-che en Sociale Geografie* 98 (2007): 545–563. https://doi.org/10.1111/j.1467-9663.2007.00425.x.

Bradley, G., 'Oil, Gas Explorer Pulls Out', *New Zealand Herald*, 5 December 2012. Available at: www.nzherald.co.nz/business/oil-gas-explorer-pulls-out/AQNMAFN2IQ2MDMR5CCOBSJUJZI/ (accessed 6 January 2016).

Bray, A., 'School Strike 4 Climate: Shifting Post-political Discourses of Youth, Climate, and Democracy', BA(Hons) dissertation, School of Geography, University of Otago, New Zealand, 2020.

Brickell, C., 'Heroes and Invaders: Gay and Lesbian Pride Parades and the Public/Private Distinction in New Zealand Media Accounts', *Gender, Place and Culture: A Journal of Feminist Geography* 7/2 (2000): 163–178. https://doi.org/10.1080/713668868.

Brock, A., '"Frack off": Towards an Anarchist Political Ecology Critique of Corporate and State Responses to Anti-Fracking Resistance in the UK', *Political Geography* 82 (2020): 102246. https://doi.org/10.1016/j.polgeo.2020.102246.

Brown, A., 'A powerful Petrochemical Lobby Group Advanced Anti-Protest Legislation in the Midst of the Pandemic', *The Intercept*, 8 June 2020. https://theintercept.com/2020/06/07/pipeline-petrochemical-lobbying-group-anti-protest-law/?utm_source=facebook&utm_medium=social&utm_campaign=theintercept&fbclid=IwAR1-j50ZLO1Zczx5zsBckN8nLLBDX2UlvYMZgbKZp5RLt4zu3trC-8QS2vc (accessed13 October 2020).

Brown, A. and Bracken, A. 'No Surrender: After Police Defend a Gas Pipeline Over Indigenous Land Rights, Protesters Shut Down Railways Across Canada', *The Intercept*, 23 February 2020, https://theintercept.com/2020/02/23/wetsuweten-protest-coastal-gaslink-pipeline/.

Brown, W., 'We are All Democrats Now...' *Theory & Event* 13/2 (2010). doi:10.1353/tae.0.0133.

Brown, W., *Undoing the Demos: Neoliberalism's Stealth Revolution* (Zone Books, 2015).

Butler, J., *Precarious Life: The Powers of Mourning and Violence* (Verso, 2004).

Byrnes, G., '"Relic of 1840" or Founding Document? The Treaty, the Tribunal and Concepts of Time', *Kotuitui NZ Journal of Social Sciences Online* 1/1 (2006): 1–12. https://doi.org/10.1080/1177083X.2006.9522407.

Cardwell, H., 'Climate Change Action and Policy Needs to Centre Māori and Pasifika Communities – Advocate', *RNZ*, 9 April 2021, www.rnz.co.nz/news/national/440114/climate-change-action-and-policy-needs-to-centre-maori-pasifika-disabled-communities-advocate (accessed 26 November 2021).

Castree, N. and Braun, B., *Social Nature: Theory, Practice and Politics* (Wiley-Blackwell, 2001).

Chapman, R., *Time of Useful Consciousness: Acting Urgently on Climate Change* (Bridget Williams Books, 2015).

Charles, A., 'Extinction Rebellion: A Short Critical Guide', *Overland*, 24 October 2019, https://overland.org.au/2019/10/extinction-rebellion-a-short-critical-guide/ (accessed 5 December 2021).

Chatterton, P., Hodkinson, S. and Pickerill, J., 'Beyond Scholar Activism: Making Strategic Interventions Inside and Outside the Neoliberal University', *Acme: An International Journal for Critical Geographies* 9/2 (2010), https://acme-journal.org/index.php/acme/article/view/868.

Chomsky, N. and Herman, E.S., *Manufacturing Consent: The Political Economy of the Mass Media* (Vintage Books, 1994).

Collins, R., 'Social Movements and the Focus of Emotional Attention', in J. Goodwin, J.M. Jasper and F. Polletta (eds), *Passionate Politics: Emotions and Social Movements* (University of Chicago Press, 2001), pp. 27–44.

Coster, A., '"We Need to Examine Our Attitudes": Andrew Coster on Policing and Racial Justice', *The Spinoff*, 18 June 2020, https://thespinoff.co.nz/society/18-06-2020/police-commissioner-andrew-coster-we-must-make-sure-we-are-not-part-of-the-problem/ (accessed 26 November 2021).

Cox, L., '"Hearts with One Purpose Alone"? Thinking Personal Sustainability in Social Movements', *Emotion, Space and Society* 2 (2009): 52–61. https://doi.org/10.1016/j.emospa.2009.05.004.

Cretney, R. and Nissen, S., 'Climate Politics Ten Years from Copenhagen: Activism, Emergencies, and Possibilities', *Women Talking Politics* 15 (2019), https://hdl.handle.net/10182/11350.

Cronon, W., 'The Trouble with Wilderness: Or, Getting Back to the Wrong Nature', *Environmental History* 1/1 (1996): 7-28.

Currie, D.E.J. 'Proposed Amendments to Crown Minerals (Permitting and Crown Land) Bill Under International Law', *Greenpeace*, 2013, www.greenpeace.org/new-zealand/Global/new-zealand/P3/publications/other/Legal_opinion_proposed_crown_minerals_act%20_amdts.pdf (accessed 25 June 2015).

Daalder, M., 'Clashes a Catalyzing Moment for NZ's Fringe', *Newsroom*, 2022, www.newsroom.co.nz/clashes-a-catalysing-moment-for-nzs-fringe (accessed 25 May 2022).

Dalby, S., *Environmental Security* (University of Minnesota Press, 2002).

Dalby, S., 'Climate Geopolitics: Securing the Global Economy', *International Politics* 52 (2015): 426–444.

Davison, I., 'Deep Sea Law "a Sledgehammer"', *New Zealand Herald*, 9 April 2013, www.nzherald.co.nz/nz/deep seas-law-a-sledgehammer/JS2BCXPI5OUNU6VOMOEGGNKJKA/ (accessed 26 November 2021).

Dhillon, J. and Parrish, W., 'Exclusive: Canada Police Prepared to Shoot Indigenous Activists, Documents Show', *The Guardian*, 20 December 2019, www.theguardian.com/world/2019/dec/20/canada-indigenous-land-defenders-police-documents (accessed 15 August 2021).

Diprose, G., Bond, S., Thomas, A.C., Barth, J. and Urquhart, H., 'The Violence of (In)action: Communities, Climate and Business-as-usual', *Community Development Journal* 52/3 (2017): 488–505. https://doi.org/10.1093/cdj/bsx023.

Diprose, G., Thomas, A.C. and Bond, S., '"It's Who We Are": Eco-nationalism and Place in Contesting Deep Sea Oil in Aotearoa New Zealand', *Kōtuitui: New Zealand Journal of Social Sciences Online* 11/2 (2016): 159–173. https://doi.org/10.1080/1177083X.2015.1134594.

Dodd, V. and Greirson, J., 'Terrorism Police List Extinction Rebellion as Extremist Ideology', *The Guardian*, 10 January 2020, www.theguardian.com/uk-news/2020/jan/10/xr-extinction-rebellion-listed-extremist-ideology-police-prevent-scheme-guidance (accessed 15 May 2021).

Dominion Post, 'Head to Head: Greenies v Oil Industry', *Dominion Post*, 25 October 2011, www.stuff.co.nz/dominion-post/comment/5844714/Head-to-head-Greenies-v-oilindustry (accessed 26 November 2021).

Donnell, H. and Cheng, D., 'Oil Giant Should Be Free to Carry Out Seismic Work – Key', *New Zealand Herald*, 11 April 2011, www.nzherald.co.nz/nz/oil-giant-should-be-free-to-carry-out-seismic-work-key/OH5GWA7N5NBFYHLX37HGHOWOTM/ (accessed 23 November 2021).

Dowler, L., Cuomo, D., Ranjbar, A.M., Laliberte, N. and Christian, J. 'Care', *Keywords in Radical Geography. Antipode at 50* (2019): 35–39.

Edwards, B., 'Political Roundup: Thompson and Clark Has Been Doing the Dirty Work of the State', *New Zealand Herald*, 22 June 2018, www.nzherald.co.nz/nz/news/article.cfm?c_id=1&objectid=12075706 (accessed 25 November 2021).

Edwards, P. and Trafford, S., 'Social Licence in New Zealand – What is It?', *Journal of the Royal Society of New Zealand* 46/3–4 (2016): 165–180. https://doi.org/10.1080/03036758.2016.1186702.

Elder, V., '"Respect" Call after Protesters Bar Entry', *Otago Daily Times*, 14 May 2016, www.odt.co.nz/news/dunedin/respect-call-after-protesters-bar-entry-video (accessed 26 November 2021).

Elkington, B., Jackson, M., Kiddle, R., Mercier, O.R., Ross, M., Smeaton, J. and Thomas, A., *Imagining Decolonisation* (Bridget Williams Books, 2020).

England, K., 'Home, Work and the Shifting Geographies of Care', *Ethics, Place and Environment* 13/2 (2010): 131–150. https://doi.org/10.1080/13668791003778826.

Erueti, A. and Pietras, J. (2013) 'Extractive Industry, Human Rights and Indigenous Rights in New Zealand's Exclusive Economic Zone', *New Zealand Yearbook of International Law* 11 (2013): 37–72, http://hdl.handle.net/2292/39396.

Espiner, G., 'How the Police Watchdog is More Secretive than the Spy Agency', *RNZ*, 2022, www.rnz.co.nz/news/in-depth/464251/how-the-police-watchdog-is-more-secretive-than-the-spy-agency (accessed 26 May 2022).

Evans, M., 'The MV *Rena*: A Case Study in the Protection of Māori Environmental Interests', an essay submitted to the Environmental Defence Society's annual essay competition, 2016, www.eds.org.nz/assets/University%20Essay%20Competition/Evans%202016.Natural%20Resource%20Law%20-Rena-grounding.pdf?k=edcda269cc (accessed 28 July 2021).

Evensen, D., 'The Rhetorical Limitations of the #FridaysForFuture Movement', *Nature: Climate Change* 9 (2019): 428–430. https://doi.org/10.1038/s41558-019-0481-1.

Feigenbaum, A., *Tear Gas: From the Battlefields of World War I to the Streets of Today* (Verso, 2017).

Filip, B., 'The Neo-Liberal Concept of Freedom: Economic and Negative Freedom', in *The Rise of Neo-liberalism and the Decline of Freedom* (Palgrave Macmillan, 2020), pp. 29–55.

Finney, C., *Black Faces, White Spaces: Reimagining the Relationship of African Americans to the Great Outdoors* (University of North Carolina Press, 2014).

Fisher, B. and Tronto, J., 'Toward a Feminist Theory of Caring', in E.K. Abel and M. Nelson (eds), *Circles of Care* (SUNY Press, 1990), pp. 36–54.

Fitzjohn, S., 'ANZ Protest and Backlash', *Fossil Fools*, 16 May 2016, https://fossilfoolsnz.wordpress.com/2016/05/16/anz-blockade-and-backlash/ (accessed 26 November2021).

Fitzmaurice, L. and Bargh, M., *Stepping Up: COVID-19 Checkpoints and Rangatiratanga* (Huia Publishers, 2022).

Fleming, Z., 'MFAT Used Thompson + Clark for Security at TPP Protest', *RNZ*, 19 April 2018a, www.radionz.co.nz/national/programmes/checkpoint/audio/2018641426/mfat-used-thompson-clark-for-security-at-tpp-protest (accessed 20 April 2018).

Fleming, Z., 'DOC Using Thompson + Clark to Monitor Anti-1080 Activists', *RNZ*, 23 April 2018b, www.radionz.co.nz/national/programmes/checkpoint/audio/2018641915/doc-using-thompson-clark-to-monitor-anti-1080-activists (accessed 24 April 2018).

Forney, K.A., Southall, B.L., Slooten, E., Dawson, S., Read, A.J., Baird, R.W. and Brownell Jr, R.L., 'Nowhere to Go: Noise Impact Assessments for Marine Mammal Populations with High Site Fidelity', *Endangered Species Research* 32 (2017): 391–413. https://doi.org/10.3354/esr00820.

Free Association, 'Antagonism, Neo-liberalism and Movements: Six Impossible Things Before Breakfast', *Antipode* 4/42 (2010): 1019–1033. https://doi.org/10.1111/j.1467-8330.2010.00786.x.

Frynas, J.G., 'The False Developmental Promise of Corporate Social Responsibility: Evidence from Multinational Oil Companies', *International Affairs* 81/3 (2005): 581–598. https://doi.org/10.1111/j.1468-2346.2005.00470.x

Geiringer, C., Higbee, P. and McLeay, E., *What's the Hurry? Urgency in the New Zealand Legislative Process, 1987–2010* (Victoria University Press, 2011).

Ginn, F., 'Extension, Subversion, Containment: Eco-nationalism and (Post)colonial Nature in Aotearoa New Zealand', *Transactions of the Institute of British Geographers* 33 (2008): 335–353. https://doi.org/10.1111/j.1475-5661.2008.00307.x.

Glazebrook, T. and Opoku, E., 'Defending the Defenders: Environmental Protectors, Climate Change and Human Rights', *Ethics and the Environment* 23/2 (2018): 83–109. https://doi.org/10.2979/ethicsenviro.23.2.05.

Godfrey, H., 'Letter: Anti-oil Protesters are Nimby Naysayers', *Dominion Post*, 27 January 2014, www.stuff.co.nz/dominion-post/comment/letters-to-the-editor/9652661/Letter-Anti-oil-protesters-are-nimby-naysayers (accessed 26 November 2021).

Green Party (NZ), 'Govt Abuses Urgency to Extend Anardarko Amendment', press release, 17 May 2013, www.scoop.co.nz/stories/PA1305/S00368/govtabusesurgency-to-extend-anadarko-amendment.htm (accessed 26 November 2021).

Hager, N., *Dirty Politics: How Attack Politics is Poisoning New Zealand's Political Environment* (Craig Potton Publishing, 2014).

Hager, N., 'School Children Targeted by Private Investigators Thompson and Clark', *RNZ*, 22 April 2021, www.rnz.co.nz/national/programmes/ morningreport/audio/2018792585/school-children-targeted-by-privateinvestigators-thompson-and-clark (accessed 26 November 2021).

Hager, N. and Burton, B., *Secrets and Lies: The Anatomy of an Anti-environmental PR Campaign* (Craig Potton Publishing, 1999).

Haines, H.H., 'Black Radicalization and the Funding of Civil Rights: 1957–1970', *Social Problems* 32/1 (1984): 31–43. https://doi.org/10.2307/800260.

Hamer, P., 'A Quarter-century of the Waitangi Tribunal: Responding to the Challenge', in J. Hayward and N.R. Wheen (eds), *The Waitangi Tribunal: Te Roopu Whakamana i Te Tiriti o Waitangi* (Bridget Williams Books, 2015), pp. 29–40.

Hancock, F. and Gover, K., *He Tirohanga ō Kawa ki Te Tiriti o Waitangi: A Guide to the Principles of the Treaty of Waitangi as Expressed by the Courts and the Waitangi Tribunal*. Te Puni Kōkiri, 2001, www.tpk.govt.nz/en/a-matou-mohiotanga/ crownmaori-relations/he-tirohanga-o-kawa-ki-te-tiriti-o-waitangi/.

Hancock, F. and Espiner, G., 'Licence to Kill: the Startling Truth about New Zealand's Fatal Police Shootings', *RNZ*, 2022, www.rnz.co.nz/programmes/ in-depth-special-projects/story/2018834464/licence-to-kill-the-startlingtruth-about-new-zealand-s-fatal-police-shootings (accessed 25 May 2022).

Handford, S. and Maeder, R., 'The Origins of School Strike 4 Climate NZ', in *Standing Up for a Sustainable World* (Edward Elgar Publishing, 2020).

Hansen, H.K. and Uldam, J., 'Corporate Social Responsibility, Corporate Surveillance and Neutralizing Corporate Resistance: On the Commodification of Risk-based Policing', in G. Barak (ed.), *The Routledge International Handbook of the Crimes of the Powerful* (Routledge, 2015), pp. 186–196.

Harvey, F., 'Trillions of Dollars Spent on Covid Recovery in Ways that Harm Environment', *The Guardian*, 15 July 2021, www.theguardian.com/ business/2021/jul/15/trillions-of-dollars-spent-on-covid-recovery-in-waysthat-harm-environment (accessed 18 July 2021).

Hau'ofa, E., 'Our Sea of Islands', *The Contemporary Pacific* 6/1 (1994): 148–161.

Hayward, J., '"Flowing from the Treaty's Words": The Principles of the Treaty of Waitangi', in J. Hayward and N.R. Wheen (eds), *The Waitangi Tribunal: Te Roopu Whakamana i Te Tiriti o Waitangi* (Bridget Williams Books, 2015), pp. 29–40.

Hayward, J., 'Treaty of Waitangi Settlements: Successful Symbolic Reparation', in J. Luetjens, M. Mintrom and P. Hart (eds), *Successful Public Policy: Lessons from Australia and New Zealand* (ANU Press, 2019), pp. 399–422.

Hiemstra, N. and Billo, E., 'Introduction to Focus Section: Feminist Research and Knowledge Production in Geography', *The Professional Geographer* 69/2 (2017): 284–290. https://doi.org/10.1080/00330124.2016.1208103.

Hill, M., 'Police Make Arrest on Protest Ship', *Stuff*, 23 April 2011, www.stuff. co.nz/national/4921260/Police-make-arrest-on-protest-ship (accessed 26 November 2021).

Hobbs, P., 'Private Investigators Thompson and Clark Unlawfully Accessed Protestors' Private Information through Motor Vehicle Register, Greenpeace Claims', *TVNZ*, 7 June 2018, www.1news.co.nz/2018/06/07/private-investigators-thompson-and-clark-unlawfully-accessed-protestors-private-information-through-motor-vehicle-register-greenpeace-claims/ (accessed 26 November 2021).

Hochschild, A.R., *The Commercialization of Intimate Life: Notes from Home and Work* (University of California Press, 2003).

Humphreys, L., 'Protestors Avoid Terrorism Conviction', *Stuff*, 14 November 2009, www.stuff.co.nz/taranaki-daily-news/news/3062451/Protesters-avoid-terrorism-conviction (accessed 25 May 2015).

Hyndman, J., 'The Securitization of Fear in Post-tsunami Sri Lanka', *Annals of the Association of American Geographers* 97/2 (2007): 361–372. https://doi.org/10.1111/j.1467-8306.2007.00542.x.

Indigenous Climate Action, 'Indigenous Response to Leaked CAPP Memo: Our Rights are Not Up for Discussion', 17 April 2020, www.indigenousclimate action.com/entries/indigenous-response-to-leaked-capp-memo (accessed 13 October 2020).

Irwin, B., 'All Charges Dropped against Wellington Weapons Expo Protesters', *NewsHub*, 23 February 2017, www.newshub.co.nz/home/new-zealand/2017/02/all-charges-dropped-against-wellington-weapons-expo-protesters.html (accessed 26 November 2021).

Ishiyama, N., 'Environmental Justice and American Indian Tribal Sovereignty: Case Study of a Land-Use Conflict in Skull Valley, Utah', *Antipode* 35/1 (2003): 119–139. https://doi.org/10.1111/1467-8330.00305.Jackson, W., 'Researching the Policed: Critical Ethnography and the Study of Protest Policing', *Policing and Society* 30/2 (2020): 169–185. DOI: 10.1080/10439463.2019.1593982.

Juris, J., 'Performing Politics: Image, Embodiment, and Affective Solidarity during Anti-corporate Globalization Protests', *Ethnography* 9 (2008): 61–97. https://doi.org/10.1177/1466138108088949.

Kay, J.B. and Mendes, K., 'Gender, Media and Protest: Changing Representations of the Suffragette Emily Wilding Davison in British Newspapers, 1913–2013', *Media History* 26/2 (2020): 137–152.

Kay, M., 'Government's Energy Strategy Released Mistakenly', *Stuff*, 4 April 2011, www.stuff.co.nz/national/politics/4843586/Governments-energy-strategy-released-mistakenly (accessed 4 November 2014).

Kelsey, J., *The New Zealand Experiment: A World Model for Structural Adjustment?* (Auckland University Press/Bridget Williams Books, 1997).

Kelsey, J. *The FIRE Economy: New Zealand's Reckoning* (Bridget Williams Books with the New Zealand Law Foundation, 2015).

Kennelly, J., "'It's This Pain in My Heart that Won't Let Me Stop": Gendered Affect, Webs of Relations, and Young Women's Activism', *Feminist Theory* 15 (2014): 241–260. https://doi.org/10.1177/1464700114544611.

Kristoffersen, B. and Young, S., 'Geographies of Security and Statehood in "Norway's Battle of the North"', *Geoforum* 41/4 (2010): 577–584.

Klein, N., 'Foreword', in E. Lubbers (ed.), *Battling Big Business: Countering Greenwash, Infiltration, and Other Forms of Corporate Bullying* (Scribe, 2002).

Lawson, V. 'Geographies of Care and Responsibility', *Annals of the Association of American Geographers* 97 (2007): 1–11. https://doi.org/10.1111/j.1467-8306.2007.00520.x.

Lee, I., 'Pasifika Bring Unique Perspective to Auckland Climate Change Protest', *1 News*, 27 September 2019, www.1news.co.nz/2019/09/27/pasifika-bring-unique-perspective-to-auckland-climate-change-protest/ (accessed 6 December 2021).

Lin, T., Protestors Rally in Auckland against ANZ's Investment in Fossil Fuels', *Stuff*, 4 May 2016, www.stuff.co.nz/business/industries/79605246/Protestors-rally-in-Auckland-against-ANZs-investment-in-fossil-fuels (accessed 9 June 2016).

Locke, K., 'Spy Chief's Apology to Me Reveals Scandalous Truth about the SIS', *The Spinoff*, 17 January 2019, https://thespinoff.co.nz/politics/17-01-2019/keith-locke-spy-chiefs-apology-to-me-reveals-scandalous-truth-about-the-sis/?fbclid=IwAR14DjTli4QjYnZliLeXZwDmHccjZh8bxLTWXnJuLFjmHqI9IG PZEcy6BGM (accessed 18 January 2019).

Loftus, B., 'Police Occupational Culture: Classic Themes, Altered Times', *Policing and Society* 20/1 (2010): 1–20, https://doi.org/10.1080/10439460903281547.

Lubbers, E., 'Undercover Research – Corporate and Police Spying on Activists. An Introduction to Activist Intelligence as A New Field of Study', *Surveillance and Society* 13/3-4 (2015): 338–353.

Lubbers, E., 'Undercover Research: Academics, Activists and Others Investigate Political Policing', in A. Choudry (ed.), *Activists and the Surveillance State: Learning from Repression* (Pluto Books, 2019), pp. 217–248.

Lyon, D., *Surveillance Society: Monitoring Everyday Life* (Open University Press, 2001).

Mann, G., 'Doom', *Keywords in Radical Geography: Antipode at 50* (2019): 90–94. https://onlinelibrary.wiley.com/doi/pdf/10.1002/9781119558071.

Martin, D. and Mount, S. QC, 'Inquiry into the Use of External Security Consultants by Government Agencies', Te Kawa Mataaho, Public Service Commission, 18 December 2018, www.publicservice.govt.nz/resources/inquiry-use-external-security-consultants-government-agencies (accessed 23 November 2021).

Massaro, V.A. and Williams, J., 'Feminist Geopolitics', *Geography Compass* 7/8 (2013): 567–577.

Matike Mai Aotearoa, 'He Whakaaro Here Whakaumu mō Aotearoa', report of Matike Mai Aotearoa – the Independent Working Group on Constitutional Transformation, 2016, https://nwo.org.nz/wp-content/uploads/2018/06/MatikeMaiAotearoa25Jan16.pdf.

Matthews, K.R., "'The Police Won't Arrest Me and It's Really Pissing Me Off'": When Police Foil Activist Strategies through Unpredictable Responses to Protest', verbal presentation, June 2021, Alternative Futures and Popular Protest Conference, Manchester, UK.

Matthews, K.R., 'Social Movements and the (Mis)use of Research: Extinction Rebellion and the 3.5% Rule', *Interface: A Journal on Social Movements* 12/1 (2020).

McGrath, M., 'COP26: Fossil Fuel Industry has Largest Delegation at Climate Summit', *BBC News*, 8 November 2021, www.bbc.com/news/science-environment-59199484 (accessed 3 December 2021).

McIntosh, T. and Workman, K., 'The Criminalisation of Poverty', in M. Rashbrooke (ed.), *Inequality: A New Zealand Crisis* (Bridget Williams Books, 2013).

McKnight, H. "'The Oceans Are Rising and So Are We'": Exploring Utopian Discourses in the School Strike For Climate Movement', *Brief Encounters* 4/1 (2020), http://orcid.org/0000-0002-4157-9659.

McNicol, H., 'Oil Search Steps Up as Sector Fights "Misconceptions"', *Stuff*, 19 September 2013, www.stuff.co.nz/business/industries/9182390/Oil-search-steps-up-as-sectorfights-misconceptions (accessed 4 March 2015).

Meese, H., Baker, T. and Sisson, A. '#WeAreBeneficiaries: Contesting Poverty Stigma Through Social Media', *Antipode* 52/4 (2020): 1152–1174, https://doi.org/10.1111/anti.12617.

Ministry for the Environment (NZ), 'Proposal for Exclusive Economic Zone Environmental Effects Legislation', Cabinet Policy Paper (Cab 07-C-0751), 2011, https://environment.govt.nz/what-government-is-doing/cabinet-papers-and-regulatory-impact-statements/proposal-for-exclusive-economic-zone-environmental-effects-legislation/ (accessed 26 November 2021).

Ministry for the Environment (NZ), 'Regulatory Impact Statement: Activity Classification of Exploration Drilling Under the Exclusive Economic Zone and Continental Shelf (Environmental Effects) Act 2012', no date, www.mfe.govt.nz/sites/default/files/ris-for-activity-classification-of-exploration-drilling-under-the-eez-act.pdf (accessed 29 June 2015).

Ministry for the Environment (NZ), *New Zealand's Greenhouse Gas Inventory 1990–2019* (Ministry for the Environment, 2021), https://environment.govt.nz/publications/new-zealands-greenhouse-gas-inventory-1990-2019/.

Ministry of Business, Innovation and Employment (MBIE) (NZ), 'Outcome of Schedule 4 Stocktake Process', 2011, www.med.govt.nz/sectors-industries/natural-resources/minerals/schedule-4-of-the-crown-minerals-act-1991/outcome-of-schedule-4-stocktake-process (accessed 18 March 2015).

Ministry of Business, Innovation and Employment (MBIE) (NZ), 'Home', no date, www.mbie.govt.nz/.

Mirowski, P. and Plehwe, D. (eds), *The Road from Mont Pèlerin: The Making of the Neoliberal Thought Collective, with a New Preface* (Harvard University Press, 2015).

Moen, S. and Lambrechts, D., 'Managing Political Risk: Corporate Social Responsibility as a Risk Mitigation Tool – A Focus on the Niger Delta, Southern Nigeria', *Africa Insight* 43/2 (2013): 90–104.

Monbiot, G., *Heat: How We Can Stop the Planet Burning* (Penguin UK, 2007).

Moon, E., 'Neoliberalism, Political Action on Climate Change and the Youth of Aotearoa New Zealand: A Space for Radical Activism', unpublished thesis, Victoria University of Wellington, 2013.

Morgan, T., 'Alienated Nature, Reified Culture: Understanding the Limits to Climate Change Responses under Existing Socio-ecological Formations', *The Political Economy of Communication* 5/1 (2017), www.polecom.org/index.php/polecom/article/view/76.

Morse, V., 'Spies Wide Shut: Responses and Resistance to the National Security State in Aotearoa New Zealand', in A. Choudry (ed.), *Activists and the Surveillance State: Learning from Repression* (Pluto Press, 2019), pp. 197–214.

Mountier, F., 'Why Have Thompson and Clark Been Allowed to Keep Spying on Us, in Your Name?', *The Spinoff*, 27 April 2018, https://thespinoff.co.nz/politics/27-04-2018/why-have-thompson-clark-been-allowed-to-keep-spying-on-us-in-your-name/ (accessed 28 November 2018).

Murdoch, S., 'External Review into How the Non-interference Provisions of the Crown Minerals Act are Effected', MBIE, 2019, www.mbie.govt.nz/assets/external-review-non-interference-provisions-crown-minerals-act.pdf (accessed 25 May 2022).

Murphy, L., 'Neoliberal Social Housing Policies, Market Logics and Social Rented Housing Reforms in New Zealand', *International Journal of Housing Policy* 20/2 (2020): 229–251. https://doi.org/10.1080/19491247.2019.1638134.

Mutu, M., 'Change, Past and Present', in M. Mulholland and V.M.H. Tawhai (eds), *Weeping Waters: The Treaty of Waitangi and Constitutional Change* (Huia Publishers, 2010).

Neilson, M., 'Police Use of Force Report: Māori Seven Times More Likely than Pākehā to Be on Receiving End', *NZ Herald*, 27 August 2020, www.nzherald.co.nz/kahu/police-use-of-force-report-maori-seven-times-more-likely-than-pakeha-to-be-on-receiving-end/F4WELSYC2KGHMPZF35NSCDNLM4/ (accessed 15 September 2021).

New Zealand Government, 'Rena Compensation Agreed', press release, 2 October 2012, www.beehive.govt.nz/release/rena-compensation-agreed.

New Zealand Herald, 'Joyce Made "Backroom Deal" Over High Seas Protest Ban – Labour', *New Zealand Herald*, 30 May 2013, www.nzherald.co.nz/nz/joyce-made-backroom-deal-over-high-seas-protest-ban-labour/6IS7EVCZXYVFKE7ZVBUVQWKJYM/ (accessed 28 November 2021).

New Zealand Herald, 'Government Probe: the SIS and Thompson and Clark Emails that Sparked an Investigation', *New Zealand Herald*, 19 June 2018, www.nzherald.co.nz/nz/news/article.cfm?c_id=1&objectid=12073878 (accessed 28 November 2018).

New Zealand Petroleum and Minerals (NZPAM), 'Mineral Ownership and Land and Mineral Status (LMS) Reports', 2013, New Zealand Petroleum and Minerals: Minerals Guidelines June 2017, www.nzpam.govt.nz/assets/

Uploads/permits/minerals-guidelines/mineral-ownership-lms-reports.pdf (accessed 28 July 2021).

Noxolo, P., Raghuram, P. and Madge, C., 'Unsettling Responsibility: Postcolonial Interventions', *Transactions of the Institute of British Geographers* 37 (2012): 418–429. https://doi.org/10.1111/j.1475-5661.2011.00474.x.

O'Brien, T., 'Social Control and Trust in the New Zealand Environmental Movement', *Journal of Sociology* 51/4 (2015): 785–798. https://doi.org/10.1177/1440783312473188.

O'Brien, T., 'Camping, Climbing Trees and Marching to Parliament: Spatial Dimensions of Environmental Protest in New Zealand', *Kōtuitui: New Zealand Journal of Social Sciences Online* 11/1 (2016): 11–22, https://doi.org/10.1080/1177083X.2015.1012170.

O'Neil, A., 'Second Day of Anadarko Oil Protest', *Dominion Post*, 24 January 2014, www.stuff.co.nz/dominion-post/news/wellington/9647052/Second-day-of-Anadarko-oilprotest (accessed 15 February 2015).

Oil Free Otago, 'Final End to Oil and Gas Exploration in the Southern Ocean', press release, *Scoop News*, 11 March 2021, www.scoop.co.nz/stories/PO2103/S00082/final-end-to-oil-and-gas-exploration-in-the-southern-ocean.htm (accessed 5 December 2021).

Oil Free Wellington, 'Oil Free Wellington Calls for End to "Anardarko Amendment"', press release, 30 May 2013, www.scoop.co.nz/stories/PO1305/S00451/oil-free-wellington-calls-for-end-to-anadarko-amendment.htm (accessed 5 May 2015).

Oosterman, J. 'Communicating for Systemic Change: Perspectives from the New Zealand Climate Movement', *Counterfutures* 5 (2018): 79–107. https://doi.org/10.26686/cf.v5i0.6397.

Otago Daily Times, 'SIS Probe into Serious Staff Misconduct', *Otago Daily Times*, 19 June 2018, www.odt.co.nz/news/national/sis-probe-serious-staff-misconduct (accessed 28 November 2018).

Otago Daily Times, 'Govt Calls for Calm after Oil Protest', *Otago Daily Times*, 10 October 2011, www.odt.co.nz/news/politics/155570/govt-calls-calm-after-oil-protest (accessed 22 September 2015).

Oxfam, 'Confronting Carbon Inequality: Putting Climate Justice at the Heart of the COVID-19 Recovery', 2020, https://oxfamilibrary.openrepository.com/bitstream/handle/10546/621052/mb-confronting-carbon-inequality-210920-en.pdf (accessed 13 October 2020).

Packard, A., 'Coal Ships Stopped. The Warriors have Risen!', The Pacific Climate Warriors, 20 October 2014, https://world.350.org/pacificwarriors/2014/10/20/coal-ships-stopped-the-warriors-have-risen/ (accessed 5 December 2021).

Pain, R., Kesby, M. and Askins, K., 'Geographies of Impact: Power, Participation and Potential', *Area* 43/2 (2011): 183–188. https://doi.org/10.1111/j.1475-4762.2010.00978.x.

Parsons, M., Fisher, K. and Crease, R.P. *Decolonising Blue Spaces in the Anthropocene: Freshwater Management in Aotearoa New Zealand* (Palgrave Macmillan, 2021).

Pasefika Proud, 'The Profile of Pacific Peoples in New Zealand', September 2016, Ministry for Social Development, Wellington. ISBN 978-0-9941414-1-5 (online); https://www.pasefikaproud.co.nz/assets/Resources-for-download/PasefikaProudResource-Pacific-peoples-paper.pdf.

Pawson, E., 'Branding Strategies and Languages of Consumption', *New Zealand Geographer* 53/2 (1997): 16–21.

Peace Movement Aotearoa, 'Act Now: Iwi Fishing Skipper Detained on Navy Warship', press release, 23 April 2011, www.scoop.co.nz/stories/PO1104/S00301/act-now-iwi-fishing-skipper-detained-on-navy-warship.htm (accessed 30 November 2021).

Peck, J., *Constructions of Neoliberal Reason* (Oxford University Press, 2010).

Peck, J. and Tickell, A., 'Neoliberalizing Space', *Antipode* 34/3 (2002): 380–404, https://doi.org/10.1111/1467-8330.00247.

Pender, N. and McMillan, P., 'SOP Sinks Mining Protesters', *New Zealand Law Society*, 2013, www.lawsociety.org.nz/lawtalk/lawtalk-archives/issue-817/sop-sinks-mining-protesters (accessed 12 January 2015).

Penfold, P. and Bingham, E., 'Police to Investigate Use of External Security Consultants', *Stuff*, 28 September 2018, www.stuff.co.nz/national/107463575/police-to-investigate-use-of-external-security-consultants (accessed 28 September 2018).

People Against Prisons Aotearoa, *Abolitionalist Demands: Toward the End of Prisons in Aotearoa* (No Pride in Prisons Press, 2016).

Perone, A.K., 'The Social Construction of Mental Illness for Lesbian, Gay, Bisexual, and Transgender Persons in the United States', *Qualitative Social Work* 13/6 (2014): 766–771. https://doi.org/10.1177/1473325014543544.

Phelan, S. and Shearer, F., 'The "Radical", the "Activist" and the Hegemonic Newspaper Articulation of the Aotearoa New Zealand Foreshore and Seabed Conflict', *Journalism Studies* 10/2 (2009): 220–237. https://doi.org/10.1080/14616700802374183.

Pickard, S., 'Excessive Force, Coercive Policing and Criminalisation of Dissent: Repressing Young People's Protest in Twenty-First Century Britain', *Revista Internacional de Sociología* 77/4 (2019): e139, https://doi.org/10.3989/ris.2019.77.4.19.002.

Plehwe, D., 'Introduction', in P. Mirowski and D. Plehwe (eds), *The Road from Mont Pèlerin: The Making of the Neoliberal Thought Collective, with a New Preface* (Harvard University Press, 2015), pp. 1–42.

PMC Editor, 'Environmental Movement Condemns Indonesia's "Betrayal of the People"', *Asia Pacific Report*, 10 October 2020, https://asiapacificreport.nz/2020/10/10/environmental-movement-condemns-indonesias-betrayal-of-the-people/ (accessed 13 October 2020).

Poata-Smith, E., 'Inequality and Māori', in M. Rashbrooke (ed.), *Inequality: A New Zealand Crisis* (Bridget Williams Books, 2013), pp. 148–158.

Prno, J. and Slocombe, D.S., 'Exploring the Origins of "Social License to Operate" in the Mining Sector: Perspectives from Governance and Sustainability Theories', *Resources Policy* 37/3 (2012): 346–357, https://doi.org/10.1016/j.resourpol.2012.04.002.

Protective Security, 'About the PSR', no date, https://protectivesecurity.govt.nz/about-the-psr/ (accessed 28 November 2018).

Puig de la Bellacasa, M.P., *Matters of Care: Speculative Ethics in More than Human Worlds* (University of Minnesota Press, 2017).

Pulido, L., 'Geographies of Race and Ethnicity 1: White Supremacy vs White Privilege in Environmental Racism Research', *Progress in Human Geography* 39/6 (2015): 809–817, https://doi.org/10.1177/0309132514563008

Raghuram, P., Madge, C. and Noxolo, P., 'Rethinking Responsibility and Care for a Postcolonial World', *Geoforum* 40 (2009): 5–13, https://doi.org/10.1016/j.geoforum.2008.07.007.

Rākete, E., 'The Whakapapa of Police Violence', *The Spinoff*, 4 June 2020, https://thespinoff.co.nz/atea/04-06-2020/the-whakapapa-of-police-violence/ (accessed 5 June 2020).

Randall, R., 'A New Climate for Psychotherapy', *Psychotherapy and Politics International* 3/3 (2005): 164–179, https://doi.org/10.1002/ppi.7.

Richards, T., 'Thou Shalt Play! What 60 Years of Controversy Over New Zealand Sport with South Africa Tells Us About Ourselves', *New Zealand Studies* 6/2 (1996): 26–33.

RNZ, 'More Claims of Spying by Thompson and Clark', *RNZ*, 21 March 2018, www.radionz.co.nz/news/national/353061/more-claims-of-spying-by-thompson-and-clark (accessed 28 November 2018).

RNZ, 'Thousands – Young and Old – Demand Government Action on Climate Change', *RNZ*, 27 September 2019, www.rnz.co.nz/news/national/399778/thousands-young-and-old-demand-government-action-on-climate-change (accessed 5 December 2021).

RNZ, 'Latest IPCC Report Reminder to Cut Emissions', *RNZ*, 10 August 2021a, www.rnz.co.nz/national/programmes/morningreport/audio/2018807573/latest-ipcc-report-reminder-to-cut-emissions-youth (accessed 6 December 2021).

RNZ, 'Māori Climate Activist Tells COP26 Challenge Modern "Colonial Project" or Be Complicit in Death', *RNZ*, 1 November 2021b, www.rnz.co.nz/news/te-manu-korihi/454669/maori-climate-activist-tells-cop26-challenge-modern-colonial-project-or-be-complicit-in-death (accessed 5 December 2021).

Robinson, J., 'Power as Friendship: Spatiality, Femininity and Noisy Surveillance', in J. Sharp, P. Routledge, C. Philo and R. Paddison (eds), *Entanglements of Power: Geographies of Domination/Resistance* (Routledge, 2000), pp. 67–92.

Roche, M., 'Protest, Police and Place: The 1981 Springbok Tour and the Production and Consumption of Social Space', *New Zealand Geographer* 53/2 (1997): 50–57, https://doi.org/10.1111/j.1745-7939.1997.tb00500.x.

Rosewarne, S., Goodman, J. and Pearse, R., *Climate Action Upsurge: The Ethnography of Climate Movement Politics* (Routledge, 2013).

Routledge, P., *Space Invaders: Radical Geographies of Protest* (Pluto Press, 2017).

Roznawska, A., 'Cop or Comrade? Accountability Deficits in Police Covert Operations Targeting Activist Groups', Victoria University of Wellington Legal Research Papers, Student and Alumni Paper Series, Student paper number

38/2019, 2019, https://papers.ssrn.com/sol3/papers.cfm?abstract_id=3485304 (accessed 19 June 2020).

Ruckstuhl, K., Carter, L., Easterbrook, L., Gorman, A.R., Rae, H., Ruru, J., Ruwhui, D., Stephenson, J., Suszko, A, Thompson-Fawcett, M. and Turner, R., *Māori and Mining*. Te Poutama Maori, University of Otago, The Māori and Mining Research Team, 2013, http://hdl.handle.net/10523/4362 (accessed 26 May 2022).

Ruckstuhl, K., Thompson-Fawcett, M. and Rae, H., 'Māori and Mining: Indigenous Perspectives on Reconceptualising and Contextualising the Social Licence to Operate', *Impact Assessment and Project Appraisal* 32/4 (2014): 304–314, https://doi.org/10.1080/14615517.2014.929782.

Ruckstuhl, K., Thompson-Fawcett, M., Carter, L., Ruwhiu, D., Stephenson, J. and Morgan, T., 'Where Go the Indigenous in the Mining Nation?', in A. Boutlon et al. (eds), *International Indigenous Development Research Conference Proceedings, 25–28 November 2014* (University of Auckland, Aotearoa New Zealand, Ngā Pae o te Māramatanga, 2015), pp. 79–86, www.maramatanga. co.nz/sites/default/files/IIDRC%202014%20Proceedings.pdf.

Ruru, J., 'First Laws: Tikanga Māori in/and the Law', *Victoria University of Wellington Law Review* 49/2 (2018): 211–228.

Satherley, D., 'Key Dismissed Anadarko Protesters as Rent-a-crowd', *3 News*, 2013, www.3news.co.nz/nznews/key-dismisses-anadarko-protesters-as-renta crowd-2013112605#axzz3ZVkYCVdo (accessed 13 May 2015).

Saunders, C., Doherty, B. and Hayes, G., 'A New Climate Movement? Extinction Rebellion's Activists in Profile', CUSP Working Paper 25, Centre for the Understanding of Sustainable Prosperity, Guildford, UK, 2020, www.cusp. ac.uk/themes/p/xr-study/.

Scheidel, A., Del Bene, D., Liu, J., Navas, G., Mingorría, S., Demaria, F., Avila, S., Roy, B., Ertör, I., Temper, L., and Martínez-Alier, J., 'Environmental Conflicts and Defenders: A Global Overview', *Global Environmental Change* 63 (2020): 102104, https://doi.org/10.1016/j.gloenvcha.2020.102104.

Schiel, D.R., Ross, P.M. and Battershill, C.N., 'Environmental Effects of the MV *Rena* Shipwreck: Cross-disciplinary Investigations of Oil and Debris Impacts on a Coastal Ecosystem', *New Zealand Journal of Marine and Freshwater Research* 50/1 (2016): 1–9, https://doi.org/10.1080/00288330.2015.1133665.

Schwartz, O., 'After the Protests, Lingering Trauma: The Scars of "Non-Lethal" Weapons', *The Guardian*, 12 August 2020, www.theguardian.com/world/2020/ aug/12/george-floyd-protests-lingering-trauma-non-lethal-weapons-scars (accessed 11 September 2020).

Scobie, M.R., Milne, M.J. and Love, T.R., 'Dissensus and Democratic Accountability in a Case of Conflict', *Accounting, Auditing and Accountability Journal* 33/5 (2020): 939–964.

Sharp, J., 'Geography and Gender: What Belongs to Feminist Geography? Emotion, Power and Change', *Progress in Human Geography* 33/1 (2009): 74–80, https://doi.org/10.1177/0309132508090440.

Smellie, P., 'At Sea with "Anadarko Amendment"', *Stuff*, 11 April 2013, www.stuff.co.nz/business/opinion-analysis/8536316/At-sea-with-Anadarko-amendment (accessed 29 July 2021).

Somerville, C., Paine, K. and Tripp, C., 'Non-notified Exploratory Drilling in the EEZ: Shutting Out the Public or a Reasonable Response?', *Resource Management Journal* (April 2014): 1–6, www.rmla.org.nz/wp-content/uploads/2016/07/rmj_april_2014.pdf.

Stauber, J.C. and Rampton, S., *Toxic Sludge is Good for You* (Common Courage Press, 1995).

Stewart, M., 'Activists Blockade Wellington ANZ Branch, Demand Fossil Fuel Divestment', *Stuff*, 11 May 2016, www.stuff.co.nz/business/79854844/activists-blockade-wellington-anz-demand-fossil-fuel-divestment (accessed 2 July 2016).

Stewart, M., 'Cost of Policing Wellington Protests is Skyrocketing', *Stuff*, 4 July 2018, www.stuff.co.nz/business/industries/105185755/cost-of-policing-wellington-protests-is-skyrocketing (accessed 4 July 2018).

Stewart-Harawira, M., 'Race and Terror in the Global Surveillance State', *The Ardent Review* 1/1 (2008): 36–40.

Stuff, 'Fossil Fuels - To Stop Drilling or Slowly Ease Off the Gas?', *Stuff*, 27 March 2018, www.stuff.co.nz/environment/102615411/fossil-fuels--to-stop-drilling-or-slowly-ease-off-the-gas (accessed 30 November 2021).

Stuff, 'Government Can Handle Oil Protestors – Key', *Stuff*, 25 November 2013, http://www.stuff.co.nz/national/9437337/Government-can-handle-oil-protesters-Key (accessed 28 November 2021).

Sullivan, H., '"Code Red for Humanity": What the Papers Say about the IPCC Report on the Climate Crisis', *The Guardian*, 10 August 2021, www.theguardian.com/environment/2021/aug/10/code-red-for-humanity-what-the-papers-say-about-the-ipcc-report-on-the-climate-crisis (accessed 3 December 2021).

Sunday Star Times, 'Private Investigators Still Digging on West Coast', *Sunday Star Times*, 31 January 2009, www.stuff.co.nz/sunday-star-times/features/feature-archive/374156/Private-investigators-still-digging-on-West-Coast (accessed 9 November 2018).

Takitimu, D.E., 'Reweaving Resistance: Building a Pan-Pacific Climate Justice Movement', panel contribution, In the Eye of the Storm: Pacific Climate Change Conference, Victoria University of Wellington, Aotearoa New Zealand, 16 February 2016.

Taylor, D., *Toxic Communities* (New York University Press, 2014).

Taylor, D.E. 'Race, Class, Gender, and American Environmentalism' (Vol. 534), US Department of Agriculture, Forest Service, Pacific Northwest Research Station, 2002, www.fs.fed.us/pnw/pubs/gtr534.pdf.

Taylor, P., 'Exclusive: Greenpeace Says it has Caught Spies in the Act', *New Zealand Herald*, 10 August 2017, www.nzherald.co.nz/nz/news/article.cfm?c_id=1&objectid=11901074. (accessed 10 December 2018).

Te Whaiti, P. and Roguski, M., *Māori Perceptions of the Police – 1998* (He Pārekereke/Victoria Link Ltd, 1998), www.police.govt.nz/sites/default/files/publications/maori-perceptions-of-police.pdf (accessed 10 August 2021).

The Maritime Executive, 'Study: Deepwater Horizon Oil Spill Larger Than Previously Thought', The Maritime Executive, 18 February 2020, www.maritime-executive.com/article/study-deepwater-horizon-oil-spill-larger-than-previously-thought (accessed 29 July 2021).

Theunissen, M., 'Anadarko Protest: Small Boat Stays in Exclusion Zone', New Zealand Herald, 25 November 2013, www.nzherald.co.nz/nz/news/article.cfm?c_id=1&objectid=11162353 (accessed 14 February 2014).

Thomas, A.C. and Bond, S., 'Reregulating for Freshwater Enclosure: A State of Exception in Canterbury, Aotearoa New Zealand', Antipode 48/3 (2016): 770–789, https://doi.org/10.1111/anti.12214.

Thomas, A., Cretney, R. and Hayward, B., 'Student Strike 4 Climate: Justice, Emergency and Citizenship', New Zealand Geographer 75/2 (2019): 96–100, https://doi.org/10.1111/nzg.12229.

Thomas, A.C., 'Imagination', Keywords in Radical Geography: Antipode at 50 (2019): 164–165, https://onlinelibrary.wiley.com/doi/pdf/10.1002/9781119558071.

Thompson and Clark, 'Thompson + Clark', no date, www.tcil.co.nz (accessed 23 April 2017).

Tronto, J.C., Caring Democracy: Markets, Equality and Justice (NYU Press, 2013).

TVNZ, 'Q&A: Transcript of Simon Bridges', TVNZ, 2013, http://tvnz.co.nz/q-and-a-news/transcript-simon-bridges-5390920 (accessed 13 January 2015).

Undercover Policing Inquiry, 'About the Inquiry', no date, www.ucpi.org.uk/about-the-inquiry/ (accessed 3 July 2020).

United Nations (UNDRIP), United Nations Declaration on the Rights of Indigenous Peoples, 2007, www.un.org/development/desa/indigenouspeoples/wp-content/uploads/sites/19/2018/11/UNDRIP_E_web.pdf (accessed 2 December 2021).

Usher, M., 'Defending and Transcending Local Identity through Environmental Discourse', Environmental Politics 22/5 (2013): 811–831, https://doi.org/10.1080/09644016.2013.765685.

Vano, L., 'Proud to Protest Climate Change for My Village and My Family', Stuff, 17 October 2019, www.stuff.co.nz/environment/climate-news/116651171/proud-to-protest-climate-change-for-my-village-and-my-family (accessed 6 December 2021).

Vidal, J., Stratton, A. and Goldenberg, S., 'Low Targets, Goals Dropped: Copenhagen Ends in Failure', The Guardian, 19 December 2009, www.theguardian.com/environment/2009/dec/18/copenhagen-deal (accessed 29 July 2021).

Wainsbrough, L., 'Less than Legal Force? An Examination of the Legal Control of the Police Use of Force in New Zealand', Auckland University Law Review 7 (2008): 176–216, https://heinonline.org/HOL/P?h=hein.journals/auck14&i=182.

Waitangi Tribunal, 'The Taranaki Report Kaupapa Tuatahi', report no. WAI143, 1996, https://forms.justice.govt.nz/search/Documents/WT/wt_DOC_68453721/Taranaki%201996.compressed.pdf (accessed 4 December 2021).

Waitangi Tribunal, 'The Petroleum Report: Taungatara-Tariki-Araukuku (Petroleum, Natural Gas and Minerals) Claim', report no. WAI796, 2003,

https://forms.justice.govt.nz/search/Documents/WT/wt_DOC_68187177/
Petroleum%20Report.pdf.

Waitangi Tribunal, 'The Report on the Management of the Petroleum Resource Taungatara-Tariki-Araukuku (Petroleum, Natural Gas and Minerals) Claim', report no. WAI796, 2011, https://forms.justice.govt.nz/search/Documents/WT/wt_DOC_68187775/PetroleumReportW.pdf.

Waitangi Tribunal, The Final Report on the MV *Rena* and Motiti Island Claims', report nos. 2391 and 2393, 2015, https://forms.justice.govt.nz/search/Documents/WT/wt_DOC_85134478/Final%20Report%20on%20the%20MV%20Rena%20W.pdf (accessed 29 July 2021).

Wakeham, P., 'Reconciling "Terror": Managing Indigenous Resistance in the Age of Apology', *American Indian Quarterly* 36/1 (2012): 1–33, https://doi.org/10.5250/amerindiquar.36.1.0001.

Watson, M., 'Government's Oil and Gas Exploration Halt was a "Kick in the Guts for Taranaki": Mayor', *Stuff*, 12 April 2018, www.stuff.co.nz/taranaki-daily-news/103037490/governments-oil-and-gas-exploration-halt-was-a-kick-in-guts-for-taranaki (accessed 30 November 2021).

Watts, M., 'Resource Curse? Governmentality, Oil and Power in the Niger Delta, Nigeria', *Geopolitics* 9/1 (2004): 50–80, https://doi.org/10.1080/14650040412331307832.

White, R., *Climate Change Criminology* (Policy Press, 2018).

Whyte, K.P., 'The Dakota Access Pipeline, Environmental Injustice, and U.S. Colonialism', *Red Ink: An International Journal of Indigenous Literature, Arts, & Humanities* 19/1 (2017a): 154–169, https://ssrn.com/abstract=2925513.

Whyte, K.P., 'What Do Indigenous Knowledge Do for Indigenous Peoples?', in K.M. Nelson and D. Shilling (eds), *Keepers of the Green World: Traditional Ecological Knowledge and Sustainability*, 2017b, https://ssrn.com/abstract=2612715.

Whyte, K.P., 'Settler Colonialism, Ecology, and Environmental Injustice', *Environment and Society* 9 (2018): 125–144, www.jstor.org/stable/26879582.

Willems-Braun, B., 'Buried Epistemologies: The Politics of Nature in (Post) colonial British Columbia', *Annals of the Association of American Geographers* 87/1 (1997): 3–31, www.jstor.org/stable/2564120.

Williams, K., Cann, G. and Rutherford, H., 'Protesters Blockade Petrol and Gas Exploration Conference in Wellington', *Stuff*, 27 March 2018, www.stuff.co.nz/business/industries/102612805/protesters-begin-blockade-of-petrol-and-gas-exploration-conference-in-wellington (accessed 25 September 2020).

Winter, C.J. 'Does Time Colonise Intergenerational Environmental Justice Theory?', *Environmental Politics* 29/2 (2020): 278–296, https://doi.org/10.1080/09644016.2019.1569745.

Wretched of the Earth, 'An Open Letter to Extinction Rebellion', *Red Pepper*, 3 May 2019, https://www.redpepper.org.uk/an-open-letter-to-extinction-rebellion/ (accessed 5 December 2021).

Wright, M.W., 'Gender and Geography: Knowledge and Activism across the Intimately Global', *Progress in Human Geography* 33/3 (2009): 379–386, https://doi.org/10.1177/0309132508090981.

Yang, G., 'Achieving Emotions in Collective Action: Emotional Processes and Movement Mobilization in the 1989 Chinese Student Movement', *The Sociological Quarterly* 41 (2000): 593–614, https://doi.org/10.1111/j.1533-8525.2000.tb00075.x.

Young, I.M., *Responsibility for Justice* (Oxford University Press, 2011).

Young, N., 'Aotearoa One Step Closer to a Safer, More Resilient Future with Surrender of Last South Island Oil Permit', *Greenpeace Aotearoa*, 10 March 2021, www.greenpeace.org/aotearoa/press-release/aotearoa-one-step-closer-to-a-safer-more-resilient-future-with-surrender-of-last-south-island-oil-permit (accessed 5 December 2021).

Zalik, A., 'Mining the Seabed, Enclosing the Area: Ocean Grabbing, Proprietary Knowledge and the Geopolitics of the Extractive Frontier Beyond National Jurisdiction', *International Social Science Journal* 68/229-230 (2018): 343–359, https://doi.org/10.1111/issj.12159.

Zapata, N.H., 'Extinction Rebellion's Long Overdue Reckoning With Race', *The Nation*, 5 October 2020, www.thenation.com/article/politics/extinction-rebellion-climate-race/ (accessed 5 December 2021).

Index

Thanks to our Patreon subscribers:

Andrew Perry
Ciaran Kane

Who have shown generosity and
comradeship in support of our publishing.

Check out the other perks you get by subscribing
to our Patreon – visit patreon.com/plutopress.
Subscriptions start from £3 a month.